GREAT
SEXPECTATIONS

GREAT SEXPECTATIONS

Finding Lasting Intimacy
in Your Marriage

Robert and Rosemary Barnes

ZondervanPublishingHouse
Grand Rapids, Michigan

A Division of HarperCollinsPublishers

Great Sexpectations
Copyright © 1996 by Robert and Rosemary Barnes

Requests for information should be addressed to:
ZondervanPublishingHouse
Grand Rapids, Michigan 49530

Library of Congress Cataloging-in-Publication Data

Barnes, Robert G., 1947–
    Great Sexpectations : finding lasting intimacy in your marriage / Robert and
Rosemary Barnes.
      p. cm.
    ISBN 0-310-20137-3
    1. Marriage—Religious aspects—Christianity. 2. Sex—Religious aspects—
Christianity. 3. Intimacy (Psychology)—Religious aspects—Christianity. I. Barnes,
Rosemary J., 1949– . II. Title.
BV835.B3445 1996
248.8 ’ 44—dc20   95-25255
                                                         CIP

All Scripture quotations, unless otherwise indicated, are taken from the *Holy Bible: New
International Version*®. NIV®. Copyright © 1973, 1978, 1984 by International Bible
Society. Used by permission of Zondervan Publishing House. All rights reserved.

Interior design by Joe Vriend

Printed in the United States of America

95 96 97 98 99 00 01 02 / ❖ DH/ 10 9 8 7 6 5 4 3 2 1

Dedicated to our children
Torrey and Robey

Our prayer for them is that they would have
the information they need to work on their marriages
and a commitment to never settle for mediocrity
in the marriage relationship

Contents

Acknowledgments

The key to starting a book is getting started on the right path with the right encouragement. Without that help it would be a long arduous road. The encouragement for this project came from our publisher, Scott Bolinder, and our editor, Sandra Vander Zicht, two very special friends. We are very grateful that they believed in us enough to be such encouraging lights.

The time to travel this writing road was made available by the staff at Sheridan House, the ministry where we have spent over twenty years working with families. The office staff made up of Bob Geissinger, Carol Stewart, Duane Siers, Paul Duame, Pam Gardella, and Linda Hedstrom said, "Go write this book. We'll handle the administration while you're working." The residential staff at the boys' homes and the girls' homes were excited about this project and took over all our responsibilities there. We remain grateful to Steve Bodnarchuk, Jeri Graumlich, Lisa Trinca, Tammy Ramey, Brian Vann, and Chris Harmon, the counselors at Sheridan House, as well as Jack and Janet Ray, Ed and Ann Mac-Dougall, Gil and Yvonne Gillmore, and John and Diane Prechtel, the houseparents for the children. With the help of Don McCulloch and Kevin Groeneveld, who took over my counseling caseload, and Lillian Hughes, my personal secretary, the time was made available to write. To the reader this may seem like an unnecessary list of names, but all those listed have been invaluable friends to this project and to us personally.

All of our other books to date have been written at a friend's cabin. This book, however, was written during the school year so we were home. We will remain eternally grateful to the Lord for providing us with such a beautiful home to write in, as well as such a beautiful marriage to walk together in. Thank you to all who have invested in our lives and the journey of this book.

Introduction

"Why is this so difficult?" a man said, while sitting in my office. "We've been married for eight years and during that time we have somehow totally misread each other sexually. I can tell from Susan's frustration that she is no longer as interested in our sexual relationship as she used to be. I don't know where we went wrong. I guess I just thought the sexual part of marriage was going to be the easiest part of married life instead of the biggest area of conflict. I sure expected something different!"

When you pick up a book to read, you have specific expectations. When it's a book about the sexual relationship in marriage, these expectations can be very strong. Some readers will be looking for a technical manual on sexual anatomy. Other readers will be more interested in the "how to's" of the sexual relationship. Throughout the following chapters we will refer those readers to many good books already written to answer those questions. This book, however, talks about the many difficult myths and false expectations that can permeate the sexual relationship in a marriage. It's a book written to help married couples take the leap from just "having sex" to the ecstasy of "making love."

The sexual relationship is a great gift from God. The Creator could have chosen to create us without any need or desire for a sexual relationship. But he didn't. God wanted a husband and a wife to enjoy each other in many special ways. One of those avenues is through the sexual expression of love.

As the husband at the beginning of this introduction explained, the sexual relationship can be a very difficult puzzle for many married couples to put together. For many it has become a relationship where one person gives and one person takes. Because one partner in the marriage is continually more fulfilled than the other, these couples believe that this is the way it must be, that a husband and a wife cannot possibly both receive great joy from the sexual part of their marriage. That's a MYTH!

The myths that permeate the sexual relationship in most marriages today can cause tremendous frustrations. The purpose of this book is to help a husband and a wife unravel these sexual myths together. This will work best if the husband and wife read aloud one chapter at a sitting and then take time for discussion.

This book should not be used as a weapon to prove a point. Don't search the pages to find an area in which you want your spouse to change and then announce, "See, I told you it was okay to do that when we make love!" To do that is to miss the whole experience of the book. More significantly, you will miss the whole experience of the sexual relationship. It's not a "get" experience; it's a "share" experience. However, before this sexual experience can be shared, the myths that interfere with it must be dealt with. The quest for each couple is to get past having sex and move on to making love. This book was written as a road map for that journey.

PART ONE

Your Expectations

CHAPTER 1

My Expectations Went Out to Lunch

I usually spend Tuesday mornings at home writing while Rosemary edits the chapter written the previous week. Tuesdays have become very special days for us as we work together, and we often end up going out to lunch.

Every now and then Tuesday has actually become a very romantic time together, especially since the children are all at school. Last Tuesday looked like it was going to become one of those days. As I was sitting in my study, I couldn't help but notice that Rosemary was not in her usual chair editing. I also noticed a very familiar fragrance. Instead of working after the kids left for school as Rosemary usually did, she was taking a bath.

She wasn't taking just any bath. By the fragrance flowing through the house, I knew she was taking a special bath, a bubble bath. This is often a signal concerning the rest of the morning's activities. The fragrance has become a sensual clue to me that a romantic interlude is on the way.

German that I am, I don't particularly like being taken away from the task that I am working on, but I don't mind this kind of break. After a few moments I got up from the computer and walked down the hall to our bedroom. Laid out on the bed were the clothes she was going to wear after the bath. Not exactly blue jeans. Lying there was a very attractive dress and some of her new lingerie.

I got the message. We weren't going to stay here. We were going to go out to a nice restaurant and then come back to our bedroom. I didn't want to ruin the surprise, so I went back to my computer and kept quiet.

Rosemary seemed to take an incredibly long time in the bath, but finally she got out and dressed. I began to realize that she really ought to be telling me about her plans for us, so I could shave and get dressed to go. I decided I'd just go ahead and get ready anyway. After showering, shaving, and splashing on cologne, I went back to the computer and acted as if I were still able to concentrate.

What seemed like hours later, Rosemary came flowing into the study all dressed up. Noticing that I too was all dressed and smelling good, she asked, "Where are you going?" It seemed rather sly of her to ask me that, but two could play this game.

"Nowhere special, why do you ask?" was my response.

"Well," she played along, "you're all dressed up. I just thought you might have some place you needed to be today."

"No," I said, thinking that this was just about enough. "I'm just waiting for a beautiful woman to ask me out to lunch."

"Oh," Rosemary said looking puzzled. "I wish I could, but I have an appointment with the gynecologist this morning."

We both just kind of looked at each other dumbfounded. Then I realized that she wasn't kidding.

"Gynecologist!" I all but screamed. "I thought you were doing all this stuff for me! I thought you were getting all dressed up for us to go out. That's why I raced in and showered and shaved. So I'd be ready when you asked."

A huge bubble had just burst. All that preparation for a doctor!

We both burst into hysterical laughter, although I must admit, she was laughing much harder than I was. I thought she was dressing to turn me on. In reality, she got all dressed and did everything she could to make her day a pleasure, since she really hates going to the gynecologist. All that was going out to lunch that day was my expectations!

As Rosemary backed out of the driveway and drove to the doctor's office, I spent twenty minutes staring out the window. How could expectations be so powerful? I was amazed at how my expectations could affect not only my thought process but also my biology. Worst of all was that those expectations had misled me.

Expectations Can Be Misleading

We've been married over two decades, and still we can pick up the wrong cues or misread each other. These things happen in every marriage. It's time for bed and a couple climbs under the sheets. Then they kiss good night.

That good-night kiss is a statement. How long you kiss or how passionately you kiss says something. Every couple has their own set of signals, or at least they think they do. These signals are further complicated by the activities that immediately preceded going to bed. There's a lot to try to read, and many times the analysis is controlled by a person's expectations.

Sometimes the kiss is simply saying "good night," and husband and wife roll back over to their accustomed sleeping positions. Nothing more was meant by this kiss.

Then there's another kind of good-night kiss, one that says, "I'm very tired but I would sure like to be in your arms for a moment or two before we roll over and go to sleep."

A third good-night kiss has deeper ramifications. It's the kiss that says, "Do you want to make love tonight? I sure do." But there's even more involved in the translation than that. It might translate, "Don't you want to make love tonight since we haven't made love in a couple of days? I'm trying to find out by the way you kiss me back."

The problem is that these three good-night kisses can almost be interchangeable. Sometimes it's hard to tell them apart, and our expectations play a big part in the way we interpret them. Her good-night kiss may just be "good night." But if he has been thinking about making love, he's hoping the kiss means that tonight is going to be a "GOOD NIGHT!" It's not because she did anything to make him think so. Rather it's because he expected it from things that took place that night.

Too Many Nonverbal Signals

"Some nights she makes me absolutely crazy." Bert spoke up when we were talking about their sexual communication. Bert and Jackie were in the counselor's office for marriage counseling. He felt like she never understood his need for more frequent sexual relations in their marriage.

"The other night, we kissed good night and it was a great kiss. Then she rolled over and went to sleep. To tell you the truth, it made me crazy. By the way she kissed me I thought we were

going to make love. How am I supposed to figure out what's
going on?" Bert exclaimed.

It's important to start by understanding our own expectations.
When we have strong personal expectations, these expectations
interfere with the way we read the signals, desires, or expectations of other people. What could be stronger than sexual expectations? The problem arises when we allow our sexual
expectations to control our thinking.

Nonverbal signals between spouses who, at a particular
moment, have sexual expectations, can easily be misread. A
friend of ours has one possible solution. Tom Nixon is a race car
driver who responds to the race track via the official's flags. A
yellow flag means slow down, a green means all clear, and the
checkered flag means you've won the race. What a clear set of
signals!

Once we joked that it would be easier to use a set of signal
flags when we went to bed at night! That way we could signal
each other our expectations for the evening. As a husband always
looking for the right message, I thought it was a very romantic
idea!

All kidding aside, we know that we're not going to be able to
use flags, signs, or placards, so we need to start learning to read
and adjust to each other's expectations.

What's in Control Here?

Either we control our expectations, or they will control us.
Imagine that good-night kiss that takes place as a couple faces
each other in bed. So often that kiss is used as a clue to discover
what a spouse wants. But the search is ruined or tainted by our
expectations. The question we are really asking is "Does my
spouse want what I want tonight?" rather than "Can I decipher
what my spouse wants to do now that we are in bed?" Our own
strong expectations affect our ability to interpret. We spend more
time feeding our expectations than we do actually trying to read
the signals.

In order to analyze and control our expectations we must recognize that they are often based on perceptions rather than on
reality. A perception is only my limited picture of the situation. It

is not a fact, nor is it necessarily the same as another person's perception of the same situation. My perceptions will shape my expectations, which will, in turn, guide my future perceptions. Only by becoming aware of this circle of cause and effect can I escape it.

Expectations Can Lead You Toward the Wrong Perceptions

Earl and Erica had worked up a little bedtime scenario. When they got undressed to go to bed, Earl thought he could tell whether Erica wanted to make love by the way she got undressed. They had a dressing room off of their master bedroom. Sometimes Erica got undressed for bed in the dressing room. Other times she got undressed right there in the bedroom.

This was nothing that they had ever talked about, but he thought that he noted something different about her when she got undressed right there in the same room with him. He perceived an attitude from her that indicated that she wanted to make love. It was nothing that was said; it was just something that he thought he could "feel." A perception.

Sometimes this perception was correct. She knew that he liked for her to undress in front of him, so some nights when she was feeling romantic, that's just what she did. Over the years these nights had imprinted on his mind certain expectations. When she got undressed in the bedroom, no matter what had taken place before they went to bed, he had expectations of making love.

This was not always the case, however. There were many nights when Erica was just too tired to step into the dressing room to undress. Her clothes were left where she stood as she crawled into bed exhausted. Her expectations were to fall asleep the minute her head hit the pillow. Earl's expectations were quite different. Although Erica thought it was obvious that she was exhausted, Earl thought it was obvious that she wanted to make love that night. Erica couldn't believe how insensitive her husband was being when he didn't notice how tired she was. Earl couldn't believe his wife would tease him like that. After all, she had gotten undressed right in front of him.

He perceived that his wife obviously wanted to make love. She perceived that her husband was being incredibly insensitive and demanding. Their very different perceptions of the same situation led them to very different expectations. Their expectations clashed, and they found themselves in conflict.

Everyone Has Expectations

Several years ago we were asked to give a marriage seminar for engaged couples. For years we have been presenting marriage seminars for married couples, but this was our first seminar for couples who were about to be married.

It was very interesting to watch them. Most of the couples sat there with their arms around each other. They weren't taking any notes, and some spent the day writing each other love notes. Each pair gave the impression that they were glad we were doing this seminar for the other couples, since the other people in the room might need this help. As for them, they were in love, so their marriage was going to be great!

These young couples had the expectation that everything was going to be just wonderful because they were so much in love. There weren't going to be any conflicts. When we talked about the fun and difficulty of figuring each other out sexually during the first decade of marriage, they looked at us as if we were obviously out of touch. How could they have sexual problems in their marriage? It was going to be unending ecstasy!

One couple asked, "What happens if you're not sexually compatible?" To which we answered, "You won't be instantly compatible with each other. No couples are. That's part of the fun, as well as part of the work of adjusting to each other."

This whole concept of having to work at figuring out the sexual part of their marriage was totally foreign to them. They had such a high level of sexual excitement and anticipation about them that sexual incompatibility was unthinkable. Their expectation was instant ecstasy.

In the following months we started getting long-distance phone calls from many tearful, young marriage partners. They couldn't imagine how their sexual expectations could be so different from their spouse's.

"You said in that seminar last summer that no one is sexually compatible with their spouse when they first get married," a young bride said. "I didn't believe it when you said it, but now I'm facing it. What I expected is so different from what Donny expected. We're both battling with unmet expectations. Are we wrong for each other?" she sobbed.

The answer to her and to all of us is a very loud no! The couple were not incompatible; their expectations were. For this reason, every couple must stop and take a look at their expectations. Regularly throughout the marriage, each spouse must answer the following questions:

1. Are my expectations about our sexual relationship realistic?
2. Are my expectations about our sexual relationship fair to my spouse?
3. Does my spouse understand my sexual expectations?
4. Do I really understand my spouse's sexual expectations?
5. What do we need to do to make this expectation puzzle fit together?
6. What is one sexual expectation that my spouse has that we are in conflict over?

Expectations come from many places, and they can be an enemy to a marriage if they are not looked at, understood, and controlled. Once that process takes place they can even add fun to the marriage. But it's important to know that the sexual relationship in a marriage is indeed an ongoing process rather than an instantaneous event. To expect anything else is unrealistic.

Summary

1. Sexual expectations can cause problems in the marriage relationship.
2. One spouse's expectations can be totally different from the other spouse's expectations of the outcome of a situation or evening.
3. Spouses get their expectations from the way they interpret things that their spouse may do.

4. These interpretations may result from misperceptions. The way one spouse interprets a good-night kiss may be very different from the way the other spouse perceives it.

5. Our sexual expectations often taint our interpretations and perceptions.

Making Sense of the Sexual Puzzle

Take time to answer the questions in the following chapters titled "Making Sense of the Sexual Puzzle." Discuss these expectations as a couple. Decide ahead of time, however, that you are going to have this discussion about expectations in order to learn rather than to demand. Listen to what the other person has to say without giving a judgment or an opinion. Spend time listening rather than demanding.

CHAPTER 2

Where Do My Expectations Come From?

I don't know where I got all these expectations about marriage. To tell you the truth, this isn't even close to what I expected," Elena began. "Billy thinks we can go all evening without talking and then end the night by making love. Where did I ever get the notion that we would spend time together first?"

Billy interrupted, "She's constantly complaining that I don't act like I 'cherish' her during the evening. Where did all this 'cherish' stuff come from? I don't even know what 'cherish' means."

Each of these two people has come into the marriage relationship with established expectations about the sexual part of their marriage. Elena expected to be "cherished" by her husband, and she expected this to precede the sexual part of their relationship. "He should want to be with me and talk with me . . . and then want to make love. I don't feel adored or appreciated by him anymore. I don't even feel respected. I just feel used."

Billy, on the other hand, saw those two parts of the relationship as being very separate. He didn't understand her need to be cherished, but he did understand his need to make love. He concentrated on the area he understood.

Elena and Billy, like every other couple, arrived at the altar toting invisible suitcases stuffed with expectations. Over the years they packed these bags with materials collected from their parents' marriages and from movies, music, friends, and other sources of cultural opinion. The contents were highly individual, so when the newlyweds heaved these suitcases onto the bed and dumped out the contents, they were asking for some surprises.

Sexpectations from Our Parents

By "sexpectations" we mean those expectations that spouses have about their sexual relationship. While we were growing up, we got our sexual information from the sources around us. Our parents are an obvious source of such information, and we often grow up expecting the same kind of relationship we observed between them.

Mary's parents kept all references to sex behind closed doors. Her mother and father never touched, hugged, or kissed each other in front of the children. In fact, they never even talked about sex with Mary and her brothers while they were growing up. The only information these children got was from the school or their friends. Mary grew up holding sex in awe, fearing what it was all about. She never really discussed with anyone how beautiful the sexual component can be in marriage.

Mary's husband was raised in a different home. Brad's parents had a very exciting and healthy sex life, and they talked to him about his sexuality from a very early age. They read books together as a family that helped explain sexuality and the special gift it is to a marriage. Brad can remember many occasions when his parents went out for a romantic dinner alone and then ended the night on the sofa bed in the den, in front of the fireplace. Once a year they went away on a second honeymoon.

But theirs was not just a special-occasion relationship. Brad's youngest brother Jimmy was appointed by his siblings as the "kiss police." Regularly Jimmy would walk into the kitchen and find his mom and dad hugging or kissing. Frequently this mom would be caught sitting on her husband's lap in the den watching television. On those occasions, little Jimmy would announce for the world to hear, "They're at it again. Mom and Dad are kissing again." In response, this mom and dad would continue to kiss even more or try to pull one of their boys into the middle of it. The children in Brad's house knew that their parents loved each other passionately. Mary and Brad grew up in very different homes. One family acted as if sex didn't exist, while the other family taught the children that their parents' sexuality was a wonderful part of the relationship. When Brad's parents went away to a hotel each year, Jimmy asked why they would waste the money going away. The middle child knowingly announced that it was so their parents could kiss all night without being bothered by the boys!

Brad expected his marriage to be full of touching, hugging, and loving. Mary thought that his actions were demeaning or cheap. "Why do we have to save all our hugs and kisses for the bedroom?" Brad asked his wife one evening. "Because that's supposed to be a very private part of our relationship," Mary responded. This sexual relationship, choked by Mary's inhibited sexpectations, frustrated both of them.

Mary's parents weren't wrong, just inhibited. Their desire for privacy left the children without any clue as to how they should respond to their own marriage partners. Mary thought Brad was too "touchy feely," as she called it. Her dad didn't act like that. Brad thought Mary was too cold. His mom aggressively sat on his dad's lap.

Dysfunctional Family Sexpectations

Some spouses come into the marriage relationship with sexpectations that are warped by a dysfunctional home. This would include a wife who thinks that sex in marriage is to be avoided or endured, or a husband who thinks that sex is to be taken or demanded.

In your own sexpectations, what is the residue from the home you grew up in? The residue might be very wonderful and fragrant. Perhaps your parents had a very healthy sexual relationship. On the other hand, perhaps you observed a painful and abusive marriage relationship. That baggage might have left you with warped sexpectations. You need to leave that baggage at the front door of your own marriage. Don't bring it into the house.

Previous experiences can lead to deeply ingrained sexpectations which can interfere with a fulfilling sexual relationship. We will explore this topic further in chapter 14.

Sexpectations from Our Culture

Our culture, like our parents' marriage, plants sexpectations in our minds. Many of these sexpectations begin fermenting long before we meet the person we're going to marry. As a young girl, I read many books with romantic men in them. They knew how to romance the lady they were pursuing in order to win her heart.

Yet these dashing figures, as romantic as they seemed, were very unrealistic.

Many of the other movies I had seen and books I had read as a little girl and during my young adult years had led me to believe that marriage and sex were beautifully intertwined with a wonderful, romantic relationship, so it was only natural that I would anticipate, and even expect, that kind of marriage.

Bob hadn't read the same type of books. In fact, he spent much of his youth either playing or watching baseball on television. The baseball games didn't take time out midway through the seventh inning to show the players interacting with their wives! The things that Bob, and most boys, watched were totally devoid of any romantic relationship.

This came into play in our marriage as we walked out of the movie theater after seeing *Somewhere in Time* and I was all but swooning! Driving home we were very quiet for a while. Finally Bob said to me, "You're awfully quiet. Is something wrong?"

"No, nothing's really wrong," I lamented. "It's just too bad it can't be like that."

"Be like what?" Bob asked.

"It's too bad people don't love each other like that," I answered, staring out the car window.

"What do you mean people can't love each other like that?" Bob shot back defensively. "Is the fact that he did something absolutely impossible, traveled back through time to find her, proof that he loved her more than I love you? Is that what you think this movie proved?"

"What if . . . ," but I thought better of asking my question. Bob hates it when I do that!

"What if what?" Bob asked. "No, go ahead and ask. I want to know."

"Well, you'll think this is ridiculous, but what if you could travel through time? Would you do it for me? Would you leave everything you have here to come back and find me?" I asked.

This was an unwinnable discussion. My romantic dreams up against his pragmatic realism. Something told me that this question would have been better left unanswered. Yet I knew he was going to answer it anyway. He answered with his old practical self. "I'd have to come back first for just a week and see if I could find a job!"

"It figures," was my response to his flippant answer.

To Bob the movie was entertainment, and weak entertainment at that. To me *Somewhere in Time* was an experience and a hope, a hope that maybe, somehow, people could have a romantic relationship. In fact, for 110 minutes I was vicariously enjoying and experiencing the romance of the couple on the screen.

Many movies today have cranked it up a notch. Moving quickly through the romantic interaction, if there is any at all, the relationship instantly becomes sexual. These movies are not only devoid of a healthy romantic relationship, they exploit sexuality. Sexual gratification is depicted as something to be pursued and taken, not as an aspect of a wonderful marriage relationship where each partner cherishes the other.

The boy growing up watching some of today's movies will quickly wonder what his new wife is talking about when she asks, "What's the problem here? How come you want to have sex, but you don't want to have a relationship?" His unspoken, yet sincere response might be, "Why is that a problem?"

Yesterday's movies and books were more explicit about the romantic aspect of the relationship. They used to spend time developing the relationship. The sexual aspect was only implied. Today's movie industry spends little or no time on the relationship and immediately moves into the sexual area. It's very confusing to a young married couple. They can't figure out what's missing. It's equally confusing to a couple who have been married for some time. They know, or at least she knows, what's missing, but they don't know how to incorporate it into the relationship.

You create your own sexpectations by the way you process the information you come across. Rosemary liked what she saw in the movies or read in her books. She began to believe that these romantic relationships were the norm.

Bob had no such information to process while growing up. Without information he simply had no expectation beyond that of his desires and biology. Put those two differing expectations together, and there's bound to be a problem.

Our Culture Markets Sexuality

One hundred years ago there was relatively little input into the sexual expectation file that each person mentally kept prior to marriage. There has always been pornography, to be sure. But in centuries past one had to work hard at finding it. Sexual input and explicitness didn't attack the general public in the same way it does today.

Today's advertising industry has mastered the marketing of sexuality. Yet, at the same time advertisers have begun marketing interpersonal relationships. If they show a young, beautiful couple having a wonderful time using a particular product, that will grab both genders.

Of course, they want us as consumers to believe that if we buy the product, we may be one step closer to the perfect relationship.

Buy another product and you could be surrounded by bikini-clad young women or be attended by great-looking guys on the beach. Such images are bound to leave us with relational residue. If I fail to achieve the same results with a certain product, I may come to believe that I'm in the wrong place. Perhaps I'm married to the wrong person. I deserve to be happy, don't I? Sound ridiculous? If such advertising wasn't attracting attention, millions of dollars wouldn't be spent to create the scenes.

Obviously, a person realizes that buying the product won't ensure that he or she will be put into the party that is pictured. However, this constant blitz of people on the screen having such a great and sensual time has to have an impact. The consumer is left to conclude, "I'm not there. I'm not in a marriage full of constant excitement like in the picture. I must be missing out somehow."

Instant Passion

The innuendoes presented by the advertising world are cranked up a notch by many screenwriters. Television and movies today often portray individuals meeting, talking, and in a matter of minutes, engaging in passionate lovemaking. Instant passion is broadcast constantly.

This is a message that will eventually leave many viewers unsatisfied. "The couples in the soap operas, sitcoms, or movies don't seem to have to work at their passion," a husband lamented to his counselor. "It just seems to happen instantaneously for them. There's some kind of chemistry in their relationship that's missing in mine."

Watching these cinematic relationships left this man with false sexpectations in his marriage. Instant passion isn't the rule in an ongoing marriage relationship, yet it was in the movies he was watching. He had experienced that passion during the first few months of his marriage and in the extramarital affair he was having.

This man had allowed the fictitious world of film to lead to very unrealistic, unfulfilled sexpectations. Because he felt unfulfilled, he was trying to live vicariously through the television relationships. And those fictitious relationships made him think he was missing something. It wasn't his marriage that had gotten him into trouble, it was his focus. He was confusing lust with sex, and sex with making love. He was confusing lust with passion and instantaneous desire with relationship. His sexpectations were out of line, and he was asking for a realignment.

These sexpectations brought on by fictitious characters must be dealt with. If you struggle with this type of false sexpectations, ask yourself, Is it just entertainment for me, or am I living out a fantasy? Does the viewing give me unrealistic sexpectations of my spouse and his or her appearance? The sexual relationship should be and can become a very exciting part of a marriage, but it can't possibly compete with lavish sets, polished lines, perfect lighting, orchestral backgrounds, and airbrushed bodies. We are surrounded by input that is destined to make us feel very unfulfilled.

Summary

1. Many of our sexpectations come from the view we had of our parents' relationship. What we observe in their lives can impact what we expect to have in our marriage.
2. Some people who grow up in damaged or dysfunctional homes have been taught a warped view of the sexual relationship. This baggage must be dealt with.

3. The media create sexual expectations that are one of the leading causes of sexual and marital dissatisfaction. Some individuals take in so much media input that they think they are missing out on something.
4. Sexpectations come from outside input all around us and must be examined. How are these areas of input affecting your own personal sexual expectations in your marriage?

Making Sense of the Sexual Puzzle

1. How would you and your spouse describe your parents' physical relationship? Talk about it and compare.
2. How much impact do you believe your television and movie viewing has on what you expect from your sexual relationship?
3. What would you say has had the biggest impact on your spouse's sexpectations?
4. What can be done to help deal with or overcome any myths you may have in your sexpectations?

CHAPTER 3

Myth: What You See Is What You Get

Melanie suffered from a very difficult, yet not uncommon problem. John, her husband, was a very committed Christian when they started dating. He wanted to stay sexually chaste until marriage because of a personal commitment he had made in his youth group. The problem was that Melanie was always so provocative when they were out on dates. She dressed and acted in such a sexy way that he eventually caved in to his already strong sexual desires.

In fact, most of the time while they were dating Melanie was the one who seemed to encourage their sexual activity. Right up to their wedding night, she was continually creating ways for them to be alone. Increasingly, they seemed to spend less and less time talking on their dates and more time in bed.

John felt like he was marrying a girl who was passionately in love with him, a girl with whom it would be very exciting to share a life of romance and intimacy. Unfortunately he found out that the premarriage Melanie responded very differently from the married Melanie. His sexpectations from their dating experience were totally wrong.

Shortly after their marriage, Melanie stopped trying to seduce her husband. Their sexual relationship became very different from the way it had been before they were married. In fact, their sexual relationship deteriorated to the point where Melanie showed almost no interest in sex at all. The more John would ask, demand, or beg, the more she turned away from him.

Expectations from the Premarriage Relationship

"I didn't get my sexual expectations from my parents or movies!" the young woman protested. "I got these expectations

31

from our dating relationship. He was very different then. The whole way he responds to me has changed."

This situation reminds me of the time I bought my first car. It appeared to be exactly what I had been dreaming about: a midnight blue convertible with a matching interior. While we were looking at it, my dad voiced a few concerns, but I was the one paying for this car, so I chose not to listen to him. My eyes did all the listening. We took it for a drive around the block, and that was all I needed. "Where do I sign?!"

The saying goes, "What you see is what you get," but I wasn't seeing very clearly, and the salesman was working very hard to let me see only what he wanted me to see. He was very pleasant and accommodating until a week after the purchase. After I brought that blue beauty home, there were some major problems with the car, and the salesman acted surprised that I wasn't aware of them when I made the purchase.

Dating is very similar to buying a car. What you see is not what you get: What you see is what I want you to see until I've made the sale. Most people put their best foot forward when they date. Each person works very hard to make sure that the things he or she does are very appealing to the other person.

He's very attentive and communicative during the dating time. He treats her like a lady and holds doors for her. He compliments her on everything she does and learns how to meet her relationship needs very creatively with romantic events such as late-night picnics.

She works very hard at always looking her best during the dating period. She would die if he ever saw her without makeup. She also works very hard to be positive and supportive about anything he does.

These gentle deceptions lead to expectations, but they also lead to sexpectations. She sees the communication of the dating period as an indicator of what the relationship will be like after the marriage. He will treat her like a queen. They will converse wonderfully and intimately and then make love.

He, on the other hand, thought that dating was a time of talking and listening so that they could get to know each other and decide whether or not they wanted to marry each other. Once married, he thinks, Why spend all that time talking and listening to each other? "After all," one husband said very coarsely, "I worked hard before the marriage to make the sale, so to speak. Now that we're married, the deal is closed. Why do I need to continue to service this account?" He wasn't even being humorous. This young man genuinely didn't know why he needed to keep dating his wife.

But Melanie Became Angry

Who would have thought this sexual shutdown would happen with Melanie? One night John decided to find out what he had done to turn off her sexual desires so dramatically. He refused to leave the living room until she told him what he had done. Their dating relationship had led him to have erotic sexpectations about their marriage. But instead, his marriage had become sexually erratic!

It took over two hours of talking and listening on John's part before Melanie finally stated that she knew there was a problem, but she really didn't know why she wasn't interested in sex like she was before they got married. "I don't know why," she sobbed, "but since we've been married, when you touch me it makes my flesh crawl. I've been having horrible flashbacks." Sobbing and gasping, Melanie finally began to talk about her childhood.

Her alcoholic stepfather had sexually molested her for many of her childhood and early teenage years. She had never told anyone about the way he would come into her bedroom at night and touch her. She lived with the paradox of both fearing him and loving him. She never could get him to love her, and she felt out of control of her own body.

When Melanie and John began dating she wanted desperately to be liked by him. She wanted to please him and earn his love. But this time she was in control of her body. She wasn't forced or obligated to use her body to win John's love. She could choose to do it. When she was dating she felt she was giving her body of her own free will.

That all changed after the wedding. Now Melanie felt as if she were obligated to have sex, even though this time it was with her husband. Once again she felt out of control of her own body and sexuality. This perception of being trapped in marital sex grew until she actually felt violated by sex with her husband. When John touched her, it was a reminder of the trauma of her childhood.

Dating had given John and Melanie very different sexpectations. He expected a very passionate and intimate married life; she expected that she would finally be able to have a legitimate sexual relationship. Both sexpectations were temporarily inaccurate because the dating process had not accounted for Melanie's childhood.

After a gut-wrenching night of talking in the living room, John held Melanie in his arms until she fell asleep. He knew enough to show his love by touching her and holding her only in non-sexual ways that night. He wanted to prove that he loved her whether or not they shared a sexual relationship. Their next step was to set an appointment with a counselor.[1]

This couple worked hard at starting their relationship all over. John learned to touch Melanie slowly, trying to sense whether or not she was receiving his touch as an invasion or as a touch of love. They talked to each other constantly. Even though John never fully understood Melanie's difficulty, it didn't matter. He never took from her sexually. They worked slowly, with Melanie taking risks at accepting sexual intimacy as a time of giving to her husband, rather than a time of giving up her personhood.

There are many Johns and Melanies out there who have endured abuse during their childhood. Because of the nature of the dating relationship, these travesties are not often discussed until after the wedding. We urge you to be honest with your partner and to seek professional help in dealing with childhood abuse.

An Unexpected Problem from Dating

Over and over in the counseling room, we have heard couples lament about a difficulty that surprised them. Many times a husband is shocked to hear that the couple's sexual activity before marriage has had an emotional impact on his wife.

Tami and Phil dated for a long time before they got married. It was her desire, no, her dream, to remain a virgin until the wedding. She had made a personal commitment to present herself at the altar as a virgin. After the engagement, however, Phil continued an ongoing campaign to convince her that she would prove her love by going to bed with him. After all, they loved each other and were going to be married in eight months anyway. What difference did it make now? Eventually she gave in to his pleadings.

Though she felt guilty about letting go of her personal commitment to stay chaste until marriage, she enjoyed this intimacy immensely. She loved making Phil so happy. This temporarily blocked out her feelings of guilt and personal betrayal.

The sex was exciting for both of them before their marriage and for the first few months after marriage. Shortly into the first year, however, after the wedding festivities and thank-you notes were done, something happened. Phil began noticing a change in his wife. She seemed to be pulling away from him. She didn't seem to be as excited about their sexual relationship. In fact, she was now making love out of obligation.

Phil expected the wedding to do nothing but improve their sex life: Tami would be even freer to express herself sexually. Tami, too, expected the wedding to free her of guilt concerning their premarital sex. The last thing they expected was for the wedding to create a problem in their sex life.

Fortunately, this couple hit their second wedding anniversary and decided to go for marriage counseling. The counseling helped each of them deal with the impact of losing a dream. Through the process, Tami was able to see that though the premarital sex might have been exciting and physically gratifying, it caused a great loss in her life. By giving in to Phil's pleadings not to wait for their wedding night, she had burst the bubble of a dream she had nurtured since childhood. Tami didn't realize that she was grieving the loss of the dream and commitment she had made to herself. Once the wedding festivities were over and things settled down, she began to feel like she had let herself down. The wedding wasn't really as momentous an occasion as she thought it would be. She didn't have that gift of her sexuality to give on her wedding night to Phil. She didn't have this gift of the first experience at the right moment to give to herself. In fact, it was Phil she was resenting for taking part in the whole process.

"That doesn't make any sense," Phil responded when he heard his wife finally figure it all out in the counseling room. "Why would she pull away from me after marriage, when it was me and not someone else she shared this with before marriage?"

In time they were both able to see that, before the wedding, they had overlooked a very crucial aspect of Tami's sexpectations. She expected to give the gift of her sexual intimacy on her wedding night. She had made a commitment to be different; she would be pure. Someday when her children asked if she was a virgin when she got married, she wanted to be able to look them right in the eye and say, "YES!"

Phil needed to understand that Tami had made a commitment not only to her future, but also to herself and her posterity. She had promised God and even asked him for help in this vow. Then to please Phil, as well as herself, she gave in too early.

Tami felt she had lost something very special. She was sorry about the loss and angry at herself and Phil. Now that they were married, every time Phil approached her sexually, Tami was reminded of this failure.

Talk, Listen, and Forgive

Phil and Tami had to come to grips with the fact that though they viewed this whole situation very differently, each had a legitimate perspective. Tami was hurting, angry, disappointed, and disillusioned about the direction their sexual relationship had taken. She was enduring their sexual relationship rather than delighting in it, as she had dreamed she would. Phil had to realize the part he played. He had to ask her to forgive him for letting his desires devastate her dreams.

Tami had to ask for Phil's forgiveness for letting him down in the area of marital sexuality. They both had to work at forgiving and being more sensitive to the other person. This understanding and acknowledgment eventually led to a whole new sexual relationship.

Tami also realized that her vow to her Lord was very significant. The fact that she had broken that vow meant that she needed to be serious about asking for God's forgiveness. Fortunately, she understood that God was ready and willing to forgive her. Once

Tami had asked in earnest, it was up to her to receive that for-giveness. She then needed to take it one step further and forgive herself. By an act of her will, she chose to forgive herself and asked God to give her the strength to continue to do so day after day.

Dating Is Not an Accurate Measuring Stick

For several reasons, what you see or sense when you date does not necessarily produce realistic sexpectations. Most dating partners are on their best behavior when they are with each other. In addition, childhood incidents may affect the way we relate to a dating partner. And unspoken, personal commitments can dis-rupt both partners' sexpectations. As Tami and Phil found out, a counselor can be a great help in getting to the bottom of issues that affect a married couple's sexual relationship.

One thing seems obvious: Dating is certainly no measuring stick for establishing sexpectations about the marriage. Couples should have great sexpectations, but they should also understand that they will have to be willing to work and learn before they can enjoy the privilege of sexual intimacy.

Summary

1. Dating generally gives inaccurate perspectives because dating partners put their best foot forward.
2. Many characteristics about a future spouse that appear during the dating process turn out to be the opposite after marriage.
3. Childhood traumas can cause a spouse to respond to sex in an inappropriate way after the wedding.
4. Sexual involvement before the wedding can cause tremen-dous problems of guilt or anger after the wedding.

Making Sense of the Sexual Puzzle

1. What about the dating process led you to expect that cer-tain things would take place after the wedding? Are they taking place? Why not?

2. What do you believe is getting in the way of your having a more exciting sexual relationship in your marriage?
3. Why is this so difficult to talk about?
4. What do you do to make your spouse feel cherished by you?

CHAPTER 4

Myth: My Spouse Responds the Same Way I Do

Why is it that Ron can go all evening without talking to me," Gwen said, "and then, at the end of the night, he acts romantic just before we're going to bed. In fact, it's even worse than that. At 10:30 he goes up to the bathroom, washes his face, puts on some cologne, and comes downstairs acting romantic. Gross me out! From dinner until bedtime I don't even exist, and then I'm his 'everything.' What does he think I am, an idiot? Why doesn't he want to be with me?"

"At least he makes an attempt," Ann cut in. "Last weekend Barry and I were driving home from a friend's house, and we were having a horrible argument. All the way home we were coming very close to screaming. He said some horrible things to me. Then to top it off, when we got into bed he reached over, put his arm around me, and asked if I felt like making love. I felt so used!

"I asked Barry how he could possibly want to make love after we had been in such a horrible argument just moments before, and he said, 'That was then. This is now. Ann, I don't see what making love has to do with our disagreement in the car. Why connect the two and ruin our night?'"

To Barry's shock he spent that night on the couch. His suggestion had seemed perfectly logical to him. But it seemed perfectly horrible to Ann.

It really doesn't matter how many times we are told—the fact that men and women approach their sexual relationship from opposite directions seems to boggle the minds of many couples. Spouses need to acknowledge that the difference is okay and then decide to learn about these differences, or the marriage will pay the penalty.

We Tend to Believe That We're the Same

We make jokes about how different men and women are, especially when it comes to their approach to sex. But too often husbands and wives approach each other without acknowledging the difference in perspective; they don't use their knowledge in their own relationship.

Even less often do couples acknowledge the beauty of our differences, differences that allow us the opportunity to come together in a marriage relationship with complementary perspectives; our emotional puzzle pieces fit together rather than simply replicate.

Of course, acknowledging differences means that we must work a lot harder at understanding our spouse. To assume that we are the same means that I can just react to my own needs and desires rather think about my spouse's needs. And even when we acknowledge the differences, it is often easier to point an accusatory finger than it is to learn. Yet we will only reach fulfillment via the more difficult path.

Learn from the Rumblings

Once when driving home from vacation, we began hearing a rumbling from the car's front end, and the steering gradually got sluggish. When Rosemary heard the rumble, she suggested that we pull in someplace and have a serviceman take a look at the car. As if I couldn't handle it! When we finally stopped, it was because the tire (whose tread had been separating for the previous two hours) burst with a noise like a gunshot! The car veered to the right, and I thought for sure we had been hit. It's not like I hadn't been warned; the signals had all been there. But because I did not attend to them, the tire exploded.

If we leave our basic differences unattended, there will be explosions. A man approaches sexual intimacy from a biological perspective. Whether or not he and his wife are getting along at the moment is irrelevant. Relationship and sex are only very loosely attached in his way of thinking.

His wife, on the other hand, views sexual intimacy as a culmination of relationship. As they relate to each other and nurture the relationship, her desire for sexual expression is enhanced. In other words, the more nurturing the relationship is that night, the more she is interested in making love.

Husbands and wives couldn't be more polarized in their approach to sex. It's no surprise that a question often asked of marriage counselors concerning sex is, "What's wrong with my spouse? We don't seem able to relate at all sexually! What can I do?" Here are four basic steps each spouse needs to follow to overcome these differences.

1. Admit the Difference

Until I acknowledge that there is a difference between me and my spouse and that the difference is good, I will never find a reason to change my attitude.

"For years I thought it was just that Marilyn was different," Alex explained at a seminar. "I thought that she was the only person who had these preconceived notions about the need to be hugged even though we weren't going to make love. The day she told me that for her, the whole marriage relationship was foreplay, I thought she was crazy. Sitting here at the seminar this weekend, listening to your wife talk, I realize that it's not just my wife who has these ideas, but women in general."

This was an important revelation for Alex. Realizing that his wife was actually typical meant that he had to reevaluate his whole approach to their sexual relationship. He could no longer just write off his "weird spouse." He now had to decide to do something about their differences.

Acknowledging sexual differences is the beginning of growth. God, in his infinite wisdom, made us different for a reason. Once each couple has been able to get past the sexpectation that they are both going to react to their relationship from the same perspective, then they can get on with learning.

2. Learn About the Differences

During the first decade of our marriage, I kept trying to tell Bob that I didn't respond to our sexual relationship the same way he did. It was all well and good to tell him, but he wondered what I responded to. He needed help in order to understand me.

"Well, you sure didn't act like you wanted to learn!" I said to him during our second decade of marriage. "I would try to tell you, ask you to read articles, and even leave articles around the house. All you did was either ignore them or use them for iced tea coasters!"

It was hard for Bob to learn about me. He first had to admit that he didn't know all that he needed to know about a woman's sexual needs, and that was more humbling than admitting he doesn't know everything about our car.

Fortunately, there are "service stations" where couples can get help with their sexual relationship. Some of the best are books and tapes. Many Christian organizations and writers offer materials about sex in marriage. Use these materials to stimulate ongoing learning and communication.

Get a book, set aside an hour a night, and read it out loud. This allows, and even encourages, conversation about the various issues of the marriage relationship. It helps the marriage grow.

One man said, "After reading your book out loud with my wife, I realized that I had never really understood the marriage relationship."

His wife responded, "But these are the very same things that I've been trying to tell you for nine years." Sometimes it helps to hear them together from a third party.

3. Listen from Your Spouse's Perspective

He was finally doing the right thing, Tom thought—reading a marriage book aloud with his wife. He could hardly wait to get to Chapter 4, "Experimenting During Lovemaking." He was eager to prove to his wife that some new twists on their love life were okay after all. But Tom was only abusing the process, using it to get what he wanted. Often we are so totally consumed by our own perspectives and needs that we choose not to hear or learn. Many people drag their spouses to marriage seminars, hoping that their partner will learn to be a better husband or wife.

Several years ago a friend, a golf pro, agreed to give me some golf lessons. Rick began with the way I held the club because he thought my grip was a disaster. This expert instructed me to hold the club in a way that seemed very awkward to me, so I mentally refused to do it. Later Rick noticed that I was moving back to my old, lazy habit of holding the club improperly. He kept trying to tell me, but I just wouldn't listen because it didn't make sense. Finally Rick asked, "Bob, do you want to improve your game or not?"

"Why?" I asked.

"Because if you don't want to listen," he explained, "I won't waste our time and ruin our relationship by trying to teach you."

I didn't listen, and my golf game is still a joke. I just didn't care. I wanted to hit the ball the way I wanted to hit the ball. Unfortunately, that's the way many couples approach learning about their sexual relationship. That's the way they've always approached it, and they're not going to change. No matter how many times he tries to tell her that he loves to see her taking her clothes off, she's just too uncomfortable. No matter how many times she tries to tell him that she needs a relationship before she feels like making love, he thinks that's just stupid and unnecessary. Neither one knows what the other really wants, and neither wants to learn.

A spouse has to decide to learn. And the best way to learn is to listen to the pro. In this case, the pro is the one who best understands your spouse's needs. And who better to explain your spouse's needs than your spouse? Your spouse has the best potential of anyone for trying to describe what his or her needs and desires are.

"We try to sit down and talk about our needs, but it either ends up in an argument, or we don't seem able to explain ourselves to each other very well," Jamison and Lori complained after a seminar.

Using outside materials such as books and tapes on the topic that you want to discuss can help each of you put your feelings into words. Read the book out loud and let it set the tone for the discussion. The important ingredient here is to listen to what the third party (in this case an author) is saying. Arguments won't happen if you both decide to listen. People get better at expressing themselves if they feel that the other person really wants to understand their point of view.

Jamison wanted his wife to be willing to experiment with oral sex. Lori found that sexual expression to be difficult. Without realizing it, they were trying to use the book they had chosen to prove their own personal point. Rather than let the book stimulate an opportunity to better understand each other, they used the book as a weapon. Finally Lori announced, "I don't care what you think the author is saying to me ... that's not me! I don't look at oral sex from a medical point of view. Please don't try to punish me with this book. It only makes me feel like withdrawing even more. Can't you just love me enough to listen? Can't you just try to understand me rather than coerce me?"

Lori's pleas finally got through. Jamison put the book down and tried to listen for the first time since they had been married. As he did, he finally realized that this was not a battle of who was right and who was wrong. Instead, they had to be willing to put aside their own individual needs and desires in an attempt to understand each other.

4. Ask for Feedback

Asking for feedback on your sexual relationship is not easy. Many people tend to be defensive: "I'm not sure I understand what you're saying about foreplay. Did you really mean to say that? If that's what you meant, I've got to tell you that it doesn't make a bit of sense to me!" Whether it makes sense or not doesn't matter. It's your spouse's opinion. And when it comes to sex, people are opinionated. Ask questions, ask for clarification, and try to understand, but don't waste time giving an opinion about your spouse's opinion. Feedback needs to be sought and given at many levels, in a way that will build the relationship rather than stifle it or hurt the other person's feelings.

Every once in a while it doesn't hurt to ask for feedback concerning areas that you are working on. "Honey, the last time we talked you said it would mean a lot to you if I would wear nightgowns that were more provocative. Do you think that I'm doing better at that?" Lori asked Jamison.

"Oh, yeah," Jamison responded. "That little nightie you wore last night was wonderful! I loved it!"

"Could you help me know that by telling me?" Lori asked. She was being very smart. She not only asked for feedback about whether she was doing better in that area, but then she went further, giving her husband feedback.

"Ever since the baby was born, I've felt kind of funny wearing a sexy nightgown. I wondered the whole night whether you liked it or not. It would mean a lot to me if, when you see me in it, you would tell me how much you like it. To hear you say I looked good would be exciting for me. Your opinion means a lot to me."

Many couples have found it helpful to ask for feedback during the act of making love. "Is this good, or am I being too quick or too rough?" Some couples find it embarrassing to ask those questions while making love, but still want to help each other. In the latter case, it can be helpful to move a spouse's hand or to slow a spouse down. When one offers to help by making a verbal comment or relocating a hand, however, it is mandatory that the other respond in a positive way. Take the advice or your mate will become very frustrated. If a man doesn't take his wife's advice, she may spend more time trying to continually communicate a need rather than experience the enjoyment.

"That's it!" Libby blurted out in the counselor's office, when the counselor was talking about communicating during the actual event of making love. "It's so frustrating when we're touching each other, you know, when we're trying to get each other excited, and I try to help Mike touch me and he ignores me."

"When?" Mike asked. "When did I ignore you?"

Looking down at the floor, Libby said softly, "When you touch my clitoris with your hand, sometimes I try to help you find it or help you touch me more gently, and you ignore me and keep using too much force. When you don't let me help, I end up concentrating on trying to get you to understand me rather than enjoying the moment. You like me to touch you vigorously and I know that, so I touch you that way. But I don't like you to touch me the same way. If you would let me help you, we'd both like it more."

So much can be communicated during the event if each spouse would only listen. It's mandatory to find a way to communicate these desires.

Assumptions Can Kill Our Sex Life

We each have assumptions about what our spouse wants or enjoys. Often those assumptions are based totally on our own areas of enjoyment, personal background, or gender likes and dislikes. When we go only on assumption, we often please only ourselves. We must decide to learn about the likes and dislikes of our spouse and then be adult enough, and in love enough, to make the necessary corrections in our approach.

It's amazing how a couple can be looking forward to building the same kind of relationship and yet be looking at the task from such different points of view. Something like this happened to some of our friends who were designing and building a house.

"How's the designing of the house coming along?" I asked Bill one night.

"It's a nightmare," he responded. "We have spent the past two nights arguing about whether or not the garage should be attached to the house. I see it as a separate building standing by itself. Darlene wants it as part of the house. We both seem to have dug in pretty deeply on this issue."

Neither was willing to listen, nor did they want to understand. They both wanted to build, but they weren't able to do it—all because they couldn't get past their own personal perspectives. Don't let that happen to your love life.

Summary

1. The genders approach the sexual part of the marriage from very different perspectives. It's not only important to know that, but it's also important to act upon this knowledge.
2. Finding a way to learn about these differences is very significant. Your spouse can help.
3. It's important to know these differences so well that a person can meet those needs whether or not the needs are understood totally.

Making Sense of the Sexual Puzzle

1. What would you say is the most significant difference between you and your spouse where your sexual relationship is concerned?

2. What area of your sexual response to your spouse do you feel you've worked the hardest to change in order to meet your spouse's needs?

3. What has been the most difficult area of difference for you to understand and overcome?

4. What area would you most like to work on with your spouse? Is this a desire of yours, or is it a desire you would like to fulfill in the life of your spouse?

CHAPTER 5

Myth: Foreplay Occurs Just Before Intercourse

When talking about sexual intercourse, the term "foreplay" refers to an action that takes place before the actual act of intercourse. Everyone knows that. The debate or conflict arises over how long before intercourse the "before play" takes place. Further, does intercourse always have to take place after "before play"?

The differing answers to these two questions often leave many wives frustrated. Husbands, being biologically and visually stimulated, don't need a significant amount of foreplay to arouse their interest in making love. A husband's biology is such that he is interested in making love with his wife at regular intervals. When that biological interval, or timing, kicks into gear he becomes sexually aroused. In other words, every two to four days (the time factor varies greatly from man to man) he is automatically stimulated by his own biology. It could even be stated that a man's own biology is a major part of his foreplay.

"That's sure a romantic thought," Elaine said as she and her husband, David, discussed their sexual conflicts with a counselor. "In other words, it has very little to do with me. It's like saying, when it's his time of the month—or the week—in this case, instead of becoming emotional, he becomes sexual. He doesn't have to do anything and I don't have to do anything. In fact, I could be nasty all day, and you're telling me he will still want to make love? That's pathetic!"

"No, that's not all there is to it," the counselor responded. "You play a very significant part in the foreplay process, Elaine."

"What should I do?" she asked. "Plot it for him on a calendar so he can know when it's his time of the week?"

"This whole biology thing might sound unromantic to you, and you may not be able to identify with it, but that doesn't make it any less real," the counselor interjected. "A wife plays a big part in the foreplay. A man is not turned on by his biology only: His wife can see to it that he gets turned on by her."

Turned On by the World

The counselor reminded David and Elaine that we live in a sexually oriented society. Men in particular are constantly urged to think about sex. It is a wise wife who decides that she wants her husband to think about her when he thinks about sex.

"How do I do that?" Elaine asked. "If men are being barraged by sexual stimuli, how can a wife compete? We are left to feel so inadequate. I can't compete with airbrushed models."

What Elaine needed to realize was whether or not she won her husband's eyes wasn't her job. Trying to get involved in the foreplay was her job.

Men are not turned on entirely by their biological foreplay. That's just the primer switch. Foreplay for the male includes additional factors such as visual stimuli. Men enjoy seeing their wives in a sexual light. Foreplay for David included watching his wife undress. The intimacy of seeing something that no one else was permitted to see was very erotic to him. Elaine's act of closing the draperies was such a picture of intimacy, which said to David, "For your eyes only."

Visual stimuli add emotion to the biology. This had been an area that David and Elaine had argued about. He wanted to be able to see his wife, but she wanted their bedroom to be totally dark, and he couldn't understand why.

"You want to know why I feel funny about your looking at my body?" Elaine asked her husband. "I'll tell you why. While we were dating, I dreamed of your wanting to see me naked. When we were first married I liked having you get excited about seeing me with my clothes off. But in those first years you never said anything nice about the way I looked. Then you began to make me feel ugly."

David started to protest, but Elaine kept right on talking. "As I had babies, my body changed. As we grew older, my body grew older. When you told me you thought I needed to take off some weight, it just made me want to put on more clothes. When you commented that you thought it would be good for me to join that aerobics class, it just made me want to put on more clothes. Every time you watch a young girl walk by or comment about a girl's body on the television, it makes me want to turn off the lights and leave them off." With this last statement the tears came pouring out, and David sat there shocked. He never dreamed that these comments he hardly remembered making had such a damaging impact. By undermining his wife's self-esteem, he had become his own worst enemy.

The pain of years of feeling inadequate came flowing out of Elaine's heart. She wanted to feel beautiful, but she felt fat and ugly. Initially she had looked to David as a mirror for positive reflection, but the rejections were too painful. It was safer not to look in that mirror. Turning off the lights saved her from trying to imagine what he was thinking.

"Ever since we started coming for marriage counseling, I've been very careful not to do those things," David interjected. "When was the last time I made a comment like that?"

David didn't understand that it didn't matter whether it had been months or even years since he had made those comments. She felt uncherished and ugly because she could not match up to his comparisons. Although he no longer made those comments, he had done nothing to rebuild her confidence in her appearance.

Foreplay Is "Always"

Then she said it: "Foreplay for you may be instantaneous, at ten o'clock at night. Foreplay for me is 'always.'"

In his frustration David finally asked the big question: "If foreplay to you isn't taking off your clothes or our petting each other, what is it? How can you possibly say that foreplay is 'always'? How can I turn you on when I'm not here? That's ridiculous to say that foreplay is 'always'! Just what do you consider foreplay?"

Just as it may have seemed ridiculous for Elaine to try to identify with the way a male became primed sexually, by his internal biology, it seemed equally ridiculous for David to identify with the female perspective. How could anybody be turned on sexually by acts or gestures that seem so unsexual? Whether or not he identified was irrelevant. What was pivotal here was that each person learn about these differences that existed in the sexual makeup of his or her spouse and that each comply with the other.

Elaine was trying to say that she couldn't separate the relationship and the marriage from the foreplay. They flow together. She was trying to tell David that the way he treated her had an impact on the way she felt about their sex life. The things he did and said all during the day were considered foreplay or, in many cases, they were like a cold shower. They turned her off.

David was surprised to find out that the day he called her from work, just to talk because he missed her, was a great turn-on to her. She labeled that as foreplay. If he returns from work, comes into the house, and gives her a hug, that's foreplay. But it must be a hug, not a grab. She often feels used when he hugs and touches her body sexually, then just walks away and doesn't talk to her. It's as if he wants something from her, but he doesn't want a relationship. She feels loved when he hugs with no strings attached.

The surprising statement to David was that it turned her on when he was loving to her all evening and then didn't approach her sexually that night. "You mean if I'm romantic and then we don't make love that night, that turns you on?" David asked his wife. But his tone said, "You can't be serious. That seems absolutely ridiculous to me. That would frustrate me."

This was so foreign to David that he thought maybe they weren't really talking about making love. After all, when you're turned on, you're turned on to go ahead and make love, aren't you?

First Love, Then Make Love

"I'll tell you what is the ultimate foreplay for me," Elaine said, "and it will probably only add to the confusion.

"You come in the door at night and give me a no-strings-attached hug. Then you say that you have already called a baby-sitter, because we are going out to dinner. When I say that I already have dinner half finished, you tell me to freeze it and go take a bath while you watch the kids. We then go out to a nice dinner, alone, and when we return home we sit in front of the fireplace and kiss. Finally, we go to bed, and (but you'll never understand this part) we fall asleep naked in each other's arms."

David listened for a moment. When he was sure he hadn't missed something, he risked asking, "That's it!? Do you really mean you wouldn't even make love that night?"

Elaine went on to explain what she meant. She said that she often felt trapped. If they had a great night together, she felt like she had no option but to "pay him" by making love. She felt that sometimes when he was nice to her it was not always for the sake of being nice, but because he wanted something from her—sex.

Elaine continued, "If we didn't make love that night, I would know that you loved me, rather than having your needs met. Feeling special is a turn-on to me."

"Turned on to do what?" David asked as he was trying to understand.

"Turned on to make love the next night or even the next morning. Turned on because I felt like I had a say in our sexual relationship. Turned on because I knew you weren't trying to manipulate me to get what you wanted. Turned on to make love, not just biological sex because you saw a naked body on television or in our bedroom. I would be turned on by the way you loved me that night. I guess that's it. Foreplay for me is the way you love me. When I first feel like I'm loved for who I am, rather than for what I will do for you at eleven o'clock, that gets me excited to make love. It's the big picture, not the ten o'clock picture. It's the whole relationship that turns me on."

Clearly there is a big difference in the way this husband and wife approach the issue of foreplay. It's a matter of educating each other. It's not a matter of agreeing and one person deciding to become like the other person. It all starts with this kind of dialogue. David and Elaine came a long way in their understanding of each other that day in the counselor's office. Now it was up to them to decide what to do with that information.

If David decided that Elaine's ideas of "whole relationship" foreplay were absolutely ridiculous, his wife would remain sexually unfulfilled. If Elaine decided that this "whole biological thing," as she called it, was disgusting, she too would only leave her husband frustrated and unhappy. They needed to listen to each other's needs and perspectives to begin responding.

But the word "respond" indicates that a person should wait for his partner to make the first move. Then he will have something that he can respond to. The question remains, what should a person do if his or her partner doesn't make *any* moves that can be responded to? Someone must risk responding to the need, rather than waiting for an overt gesture.

Summary

1. Foreplay is a confusing preamble to the physical sexual experience.
2. Most men would describe foreplay as the arousing interplay that takes place shortly before intercourse.
3. Most women would describe foreplay as a behavior that takes place throughout the whole marital relationship.
4. A conflict arises when spouses don't understand or talk about the large gap between these two definitions.

Making Sense of the Sexual Puzzle

1. How would you describe your spouse's likes and dislikes concerning sexual foreplay?
2. How would you describe your own likes and dislikes concerning sexual foreplay?
3. What is it about your approach to foreplay that causes the most conflict in your marriage?
4. What could you do to improve your approach to foreplay in your marriage?

CHAPTER 6
Myth: I Can't Respond to Nothing

I appreciate hearing information that will help us respond to each other, but what if I'm the only one responding?" Glen asked me after a marriage seminar. "This weekend has been very helpful when it comes to teaching us ways to respond to our spouses when they interact with us sexually. It's helpful to be able to interpret what a spouse is really saying or doing. But what if your spouse makes no sexual advances whatsoever? What if a spouse seems to have no interest at all in a sexual relationship in the marriage? It's hard to respond when there's nothing to respond to!"

The word *respond* implies a prior action. It's a reply. If someone takes a swing at me, my natural response is to duck or to move out of the way. If someone reaches out to shake hands with me, my natural response is to reach out and shake hands with him.

It's natural to respond to action that is taken toward you. But what if no action is taken? What happens if a marriage has reached a point where one spouse has shut down sexually or views sex as something that must be endured rather than enjoyed, something that they would never initiate? Can spouses respond to their mates when no romantic or sexual action is ever initiated?

Doing What Comes Naturally Doesn't Always Work

I grew up in the northeastern part of the United States. People in that part of the country don't typically go out of their way to say hi to strangers. It was quite a transition for me to go to college in a small town in the South. Walking down the street in that small town or on that small college campus meant saying hi to everyone you passed. Even though people didn't know you, they said, "Hi!" or nodded when they passed you on the street. It was just natural. I had to learn to respond to their greetings or I would have been branded a snob.

After college, we moved to southeast Florida. South Florida is filled with people who are northeastern transplants. Many people pass each other on the street and don't even make eye contact, let alone say hi. I had to get used to not having anything to respond to. After several months of greeting passing strangers and getting a blank stare from them, I discontinued the practice of greeting people I didn't know. Why initiate anything? They weren't going to respond anyway.

I soon realized that I had allowed myself to be controlled by the people around me. I had allowed the unfriendliness of this area to change my reaction to seeing someone walk by me. After speaking in North Carolina one weekend, I quickly fell back into the southern habit of greeting people as I passed them. I decided that I was going to take this custom back to south Florida.

Once again, I greet people when I pass them. In some cases women respond by grabbing their purses, and mothers reach to protect their small children from this "weirdo" who says hi. People aren't accustomed to this kind of familiarity, but I have decided that it doesn't matter. Rather than wait for a "community spirit" to emerge, I am responding to my own desire to have a community.

A key concept here is "doing what comes naturally." People naturally respond to actions taken toward them. When no action is taken, no response is generated.

Sometimes a spouse must do the unnatural and respond to an unresponsive husband or wife.

Respond to Your Own Needs

"But how long do I initiate before I give up?" Glen asked. "When do I just say I'm tired of being the one to always initiate our sex life and get little or nothing in return? When do I quit trying?"

"When you lose the desire," the speaker responded.

"I'll never lose the desire," Glen shot back, "though it would be easier if I didn't have the desire anymore. Then this wouldn't cause such a conflict. We could both just go through life and pass each other in the hall without even touching!"

The more Glen told me, the more I realized that he was trying to change his spouse rather than change his approach. The harder he tried to change his spouse, the more she resisted or gave in to sex with an obligatory attitude. The more he complained, the less she wanted to talk about it. He was reacting to her, and he found that he was pushing her away. Actually, he was reacting to what he wanted her to be, rather than to who she was at the moment. It wasn't working, and they were both unhappy.

In another marriage, Nancy wanted romance. She longed for her husband, Larry, to come home with flowers and turn on soft music after the kids were in bed. Instead, he came home in his smelly workout clothes, and when the kids were in bed, he turned on the ball game instead of the romantic music. He never caught the hints that she left, so she decided to meet her need herself.

No, it wasn't the same as it could have been if her husband had initiated the romantic scene, but she decided that she wanted flowers around her house enough to make the purchase herself. It made her feel more romantic to be in that atmosphere, and it was an opportunity to illustrate for him what she liked. The soft music was always her idea. Even though she asked Larry if he minded that she played the soft music while they ate dinner or sat in the den reading, she got part of her wish. Her need included feeling like a lady and having these trappings of music and flowers around her.

Nancy made the decision to meet a few of her own needs. She did so in a way that would be instructional to Larry and yet not make him feel inadequate. She didn't do it in a way that could be interpreted to say, "You idiot! Can't you see you're supposed to be doing this!" She just did it. Over a period of years Larry began to take the hint and pick up the flowers for her. He even began to turn on her favorite classical radio station at dinnertime.

Nancy found the boundary line. She met some of her own needs. She didn't sit and pine away waiting for her husband to do these things. She didn't ask him over and over. She did not do these things with ulterior motives. She was patiently waiting for Larry to willingly step farther into her world, and she was always careful not to make him feel inadequate.

Glen Went Over the Boundary Line

Glen also decided to start responding to his own needs. He decided that whether or not his wife wanted affection, he was going to initiate it. The problem with Glen's approach to responding to his needs was that he crossed some sensitive boundaries inside his wife.

Glen sat next to her while watching a television program and put his arm around her. This gesture met his need for close proximity without violating his wife's space. That done over a long period of time could have allowed his wife the opportunity to get used to the affection and the idea that Glen just wanted to hold her.

Glen's wife had become cold toward him for a reason. There was a reason why she never initiated sex and was unresponsive. Whether or not Glen knew that reason was not the issue here. He had to balance his need for affection with the fact that she wanted her own space.

The next steps that Glen took were exactly what his wife expected. She could get used to an affectionate arm around her while watching television. But she had learned to hold herself rigid waiting for what came next. Before long he was holding her closer and putting his hand in her blouse.

"But I thought that I was just responding to my needs," Glen commented to the counselor. "It was a disaster. She said to me that all I ever wanted was to take from her rather than give to her! The next thing I knew we were screaming at each other. Before she stormed out of the room she said, 'I could be a corpse and you'd still grab at my body!'"

The Boundary Is Real

Glen didn't understand his wife's boundaries. He was also more concerned about meeting short-term needs (that particular night) than making long-term marital gains. It's a step-by-step process that requires patience and asks for nothing in return.

Find the Balance

Responding to your own personal needs involves a balancing factor. The action taken needs to stop short of alienating a spouse. "I knew it!" Glen's wife probably thought. "He doesn't have his arm around me to be affectionate. This is just his first move."

Glen had the desire to be intimate with his wife. But he was operating on his definition of intimacy rather than hers. If Glen had taken the time to discover how his wife needed to experience intimacy, he might have been able to dismantle the boundary wall slowly, gently, brick by brick. Instead, he attacked the wall with plastic explosives, and his demolition project failed miserably.

Glen felt that his biological needs should take precedence over his wife's sexual indifference. He wanted to debate that issue in order to find out who was "right." But it wasn't a matter of who was right. In fact, the very debate or conflict was never going to be "won." Both Glen and his wife were already losing, and if only one of them were to win, the other would still be losing. Because they were so opposed to each other's approach to their sexual relationship, they were missing an opportunity to share the win.

Give a Reply to Your Spouse's Silence

Perhaps a spouse is silent because she is afraid to risk intimacy, afraid that too much will be expected of her. If a spouse isn't giving any sexual signals to respond to, perhaps that means to go, but go slowly. Go forward without expecting to reach any goals.

"Every time we sit next to each other on the couch, Glen acts like it's time to start pawing me. I'd like to sit next to him, but it's just easier to stay away. That's why I sit alone in the chair."

The silence or nonresponsiveness means something, perhaps the presence of a past pain or a lack of understanding. It may indicate a physical pain. It may mean that one spouse feels used by the other. Finding the limit of how far to step into a spouse's sexual space means proceeding very slowly. Take note of the response, if any. Glen's wife just sat and waited for him to go for broke and meet his own needs. She was unable to enjoy an intimate time with him because she felt there was never anything in it for her. When Glen finally decided to just be affectionate for several weeks without any strings attached, it opened the door for them to start talking. Glen risked meeting some of his own needs for affection, but he also learned to stop short of going over his wife's boundaries. She, in turn, was able to step closer to her boundaries and risk. She knew she was free to back away if she needed to, so she felt protected rather than used.

Nancy, the other wife mentioned earlier, stopped waiting for her husband to supply her with flowers and soft music. She didn't make him feel bad; she just went ahead and got them anyway. Eventually he started doing those things himself.

Both of these spouses had to decide to respond to some of their own needs without going over the boundaries of their husband or wife. Instead of moping around wishing they had this or did that, they made an effort. But they had to respect their spouse's territory. Eventually their spouse stepped out from behind the "brick wall." With one of these marriages it took many months. With the other it took years. No positive changes would have been made, however, unless Glen and Nancy decided to stop complaining and start responding to their spouses.

Summary

1. Decide to respond to some of your own needs. Don't sit and wait for your spouse to act spontaneously.
2. For those who have a sexually unresponsive spouse, learn the boundary lines.
3. Be patient as you take action. Go for long-term gains.
4. The unresponsive spouse became that way for a reason. It takes time to pull down those walls.

Making Sense of the Sexual Puzzle

1. Why is it that my spouse seems unresponsive to me sexually?
2. What have I done to hinder my spouse's sexual responses to me?
3. What can I do differently to help my spouse be more comfortable in our sexual relationship?
4. What would be a step I would most like my spouse to take concerning our sexual relationship? What is it that I know my spouse would most like me to do concerning our sexual relationship?

CHAPTER 7

Myth: Good Sex Is When You Fill My Wish List

It doesn't seem to matter what I agree to do. My husband seems to keep adding to his sexual wish list." Fran exhaled in frustration. "It's as if nothing's ever quite enough! Just as soon as I agree to try something that I really don't want to do, he comes up with another new and different thing for us to try. I quit! We've long since gone over the line, as far as I'm concerned! I've finally realized that I will never be able to totally satisfy him in our sex life. So I've quit trying."

The Ongoing List

Many spouses develop a list of sexual activities that they would like to do or experiment with. There's nothing wrong with being creative, as long as both spouses are interested in being creative. The key to the whole sexual adventure is that the couple be in agreement about what they do.

As has been stated, the plan for sexual intimacy in marriage is to become *one* in the adventure. Trying to get a spouse to do something that he or she is opposed to, or feels degraded by, is to *take* from a spouse, rather than to *share* with a spouse. Sex is not what one spouse can get another spouse to do; sex is what a couple can do together.

Those who enter the sexual adventure in order to *get* from a spouse will find themselves in a battle. "Oh, give me a break," Ron said to the counselor, as he sat in his office. "Do you mean to tell me that you see sex with your wife as a great opportunity to bring her happiness? That you don't think about your needs but only her needs? That sounds nice in theory, but in reality that doesn't seem very natural!"

That's exactly right. It's not at all natural to focus on another person's happiness over our own, especially in a sexual relationship. The potential for such a great "get" leads a person to pursue his or her own wants, rather than the wants of a spouse. But we are called to do what may seem unnatural. Two people *give in* for the happiness of the other person. They meet the wants of a spouse while helping a spouse understand their wants. When two people pursue the good of the other person first, they will be drawn closer to each other. Giving will be the catalyst to make both people much happier and more satisfied. Although this method takes longer, it brings more lasting happiness.

Cherish the Challenge Versus Cherish the Spouse

Where do we even get the ideas and fantasies that pop into our heads? Where does a woman come up with the idea of a candlelight dinner on a blanket, next to a pond, with her husband singing a love song? Where does a man come up with the idea of watching a sexually explicit video while he makes love with his wife?

Many women who just read that last paragraph are now thinking that that particular female fantasy and that particular male fantasy shouldn't even be linked together in the same paragraph. "How could anybody compare the beauty of a moonlit night, listening to my husband sing a love song by a pond with something as unromantic as watching two actors having sex? Those two illustrations are not even close!" She sees the first picture as beautiful, while she sees the latter as disgusting. Some men who read that same paragraph might feel just the opposite.

Over and over again there are couples visiting counselors with items on their sexual list that their spouse finds unacceptable. Some are even unbiblical and immoral. Yet couples argue over these issues and try to make demands on each other that destroy intimacy. When one spouse feels that the desires on his or her particular wish list are mandatory for happiness, the other person may begin to feel used rather than cherished. Sexual intimacy in the marriage is either a shared adventure, or it is an obligation. If one spouse takes while the other spouse endures, the latter will very quickly become disenchanted with the whole sexual experience.

In this era of individual rights, many people have been raised to pursue the challenges of life rather than to cherish the relationships of life. They wonder, How much can I get other people to *do* for me? Some people enjoy pursuing the prize more than the prize itself. Once the prize is obtained, they become disenchanted with it: That "perhaps there's something more out there" thinking can lead to discontentment.

Some spouses seem to cherish the challenge of trying to get a spouse to do something new and different even more than they cherish the actual sexual relationship. They like the thought of being in control and being able to coerce a spouse to do something for them, especially if it's something that a spouse doesn't want to do. Creativity is not the issue. Once again, the question to be answered is, Why I am really asking my spouse to do this? Is it to further conquer a spouse? To see if I can get my spouse to do something he or she is not comfortable doing? Or is it for the sake of the relationship?

If the relationship is of primary importance and my spouse finds the activity objectionable, then I will quickly back away so as not to harm the relationship. End of debate! Not worth mentioning again! Not worth destroying the "one fleshness" that we are all striving for. Ultimately the question is, Will this make *us* happy?

Eric was a husband who spent many years living with this problem. He was constantly coercing Connie into trying new things. At first they were fun things that they both enjoyed, things such as new sexual positions or making love in different rooms of the house. Connie found that these early suggestions from Eric were adding excitement to their relationship. Those items on the wish list became shared items.

From there, however, Eric moved on to wanting to watch R-rated videos with sexually explicit scenes. Connie no longer shared these wishes. She knew they were not the right thing to give in to, but she felt stuck. Wasn't she supposed to please her husband? Then, after Connie finally agreed to try the R-rated videos, it wasn't long until Eric was bringing home X-rated videos. Eric was continually pushing just a little farther, so that their sexual relationship became an ongoing battle of wills.

Eric started by bringing other women into his bedroom via the videos. One day, Connie, a flight attendant, came home early

from a canceled flight only to find that Eric was no longer bringing videos home. Now he was bringing another woman home.

Eric had become addicted to the challenge. He had made the
choice of getting excited about doing what he hadn't done yet.
In so doing, he destroyed the potential for real happiness and
intimacy.

"I don't know how it ever went this far." Eric, now broken, sat
weeping in the counselor's office. "The thing I really wanted the
most was Connie. Now with this passion for trying new things,
I've allowed myself to destroy the intimacy in my marriage."

The Battle Over Oral Sex

Ben wanted Joann to "prove that she loved him" by giving in
to oral sex. Over and over he had asked, begged, cajoled, and
used any other approach he could think of to get his wife to give
in on this issue. Joann, on the other hand, thought oral sex was
demeaning to the beauty of the lovemaking process.

It became a constant area of conflict in their bedroom, and it
cost them the beauty of the experience. Some nights Joann would
give in and do something she didn't want to do. She would participate in oral sex, which would destroy her romantic mood. She
might have made Ben happy, but she felt robbed. Other nights,
when Joann refused to participate in oral sex, the arguments once
again ruined the whole event. Ben was hurt that she wouldn't do
what seemed to him a very small request. He led her to believe
that she was not able to please him unless she did the things he
asked. When she refused, she obviously wasn't pleasing him, so
she felt inadequate and unappealing.

Finally, they reached a point where Joann was losing interest
in sex altogether. "Why should I keep falling into the same pit,
feeling as if I'm not meeting my husband's needs?" she reasoned.
"It's not worth the constant battle and frustration of getting all
excited only to be let down again."

The more Joann pulled away, the more Ben pushed. When
Ben got his hands on a book about sex in marriage, the first thing
he did was check the index for "oral sex." Sure enough, it was
there. "See!" he announced triumphantly, as an indictment of her
lack of willingness to try something. "It says here in this marriage

book that oral sex is healthy and commonly practiced by couples." His implication to Joann was, What's wrong with you? Obviously you don't love me.

Ben and Joann were both very wrong in their approach. They became frustrated because they were both missing the point. The question to ask is not, Is oral sex okay? or, Why would my spouse want me to do that? or even, Is it healthy? Those are worthy questions to be asking, but they aren't the key.

You don't just try out sexual practices as if they were broccoli or Brussels sprouts. Some things to some people—like oral sex to Joann—are an incredibly personal issue. And using biological facts as proof that there is something wrong with an unwilling spouse only retards a couple's sexual intimacy.

Getting the Facts

For couples trying to uncover God's plan for areas such as oral sex, few books act as a better guide than Clifford and Joyce Penner's *The Gift of Sex*.[1] The Penners begin by saying that there is no question they are asked more frequently than the question about oral sex.

The Penners break the question down into three categories: Is it natural? Is it clean? Is it right?

Is it natural to use our mouths to please our spouses? Is it natural to use the mouth and tongue to excite a spouse's genital area during foreplay and/or to bring pleasure right up through orgasm? To tackle that question one would need to look at what the author of sexuality has to say.

Many interpret passages in the Song of Songs (4:16; 5:1; etc.) as a direct reference to oral sex. They believe that there is reference in these passages to oral involvement in the sexual experience, to every area of the body—a spouse's lips, neck, breasts, stomach, legs, and genitals.

Is this an indication that oral sex is natural? It is at least an indication that oral sex *can* be acceptable. What is natural here is the fact that this couple is seeking to bring pleasure to each other. What appears to be natural in this biblical text on sex in marriage is that the focus is on the other person. The pair appear to be trying to make each other happy rather than to make their own demands.

The Penners point out that some have felt that a case could be built that oral sex is not right because it is not healthy. As a matter of medical fact, the genital areas of the body are actually cleaner than the mouth. A person who is clean and without infection is cleaner in the genital area than on the lips where he or she kisses. Cleanliness is not the issue.

What about the question, Is it right? The search for right is a search that must again encompass the mandates from the Bible. The Bible, however, does not make a direct reference to oral sex as a yes-or-no activity. It is neither denied to nor required of the husband-and-wife relationship. In fact, the Bible appears more concerned with the attitude toward oral sex than the act itself. The references in Song of Songs lead one to believe that this is an area that a couple *may* explore together if it is done for the happiness of the other person. Our love for each other should force us to search each other for this particular answer. Sexual pleasure should be a gift, not a demand.

The Penners sum up their discourse on oral sex with an excellent statement. It is important when husbands and wives discuss oral sex to do so without involving themselves in myths and inaccuracies about this area of sexual interplay. It is more important, however, to understand that "because something is not wrong, dirty or unnatural does not make it right, natural or necessary for you personally." It's important to start with the facts. That way a couple can stop spending their time looking for information that will validate their personal points of view. When one spouse wins and the other loses in such contests, the intimacy of the marriage is broken, and both spouses ultimately lose.

A Barrier to Intimacy

"But she has hardly ever tried it!" Ben said in frustration. "How could she possibly know she doesn't like it if she won't give it a chance?"

Ben had allowed himself to get so frustrated over the issue of oral sex that it became more important than sex itself. It became such a challenge that Joann was made to feel as if her desires were totally irrelevant. For her the issue was no longer oral sex. Instead, the battle was making her feel used and dirty, not because of the oral sex, but because of the attitude Ben had toward her opinion when they made love. He wanted this, and he was going to do everything he could to get her to do it.

Many couples enjoy oral sex as a very exciting part of their sexual relationship. The recent nationally touted research project on sexual behavior in America indicated that about one fourth of America's marriage partners engage in oral sex.[2]

To other marriages, however, oral sex can be an enslavement. This was the case with Ben and Joann. For a season Ben felt like Joann was finally seeing things his way. But she wasn't. She just got tired of arguing. It was a short-term victory since Joann slowly began to become altogether disenchanted with making love. She didn't feel like they were making love. She felt used and without a say in their sex life. Ben's short-term victory crumbled into total defeat. Not only did they hit a point where they no longer participated in oral sex, they hit a point where there was no sex at all.

It's Not Always the Man with the Wish List

Darla was the partner with the drive to force her husband to try new things. For her, the excitement was in getting him to do things he really didn't want to do. She needed something to "calm her down." It started with a habit of drinking wine before they made love. Then it moved on to other substances until, over a period of years, they reached a point where they were using illegal substances to "calm them down" before they made love. It wasn't even the drugs that initially turned Darla on. It was this mental list she had developed to see just how much she could get her husband to do for her. Darla's husband was a leader in their community and she knew it would end his influence if he was ever caught making these purchases for her. She wanted him to "prove his love for her" by doing these things he really didn't want to do.

Both genders can find their sex lives dominated by a wish list. This list is continually pushed in a spouse's face as a way of testing "if you really love me."

Another wife made her husband feel as if he could not really make her happy or turned on unless he bought her something. They were already in tremendous debt, but she pressed, "If we had lots of extra money, then your gifts wouldn't be as valuable. This only proves just how special I am to you!" On one hand, this man could barely afford the things that they had. On the other hand, his wife seemed to have an ever-increasing list of things that she needed to feel happy and fulfilled. He felt as if they could never get ahead, let alone win.

Where Do These Fantasies Come From?

Fantasies come from much the same place as do our marital expectations, as we discussed in the second chapter. Ongoing sexual input saturates our society today, leading many married partners to believe that they are missing out on something. What starts as a fantasy can quickly grow up to become an expectation—from "I wish" to "I deserve."

Watch enough television and you will believe that new and different is the route to go for happiness. If you just have this item, you'll find happiness. Just try this sexual activity and you'll be ecstatic. Videos and magazines get their viewers to focus on the activities of sex rather than the intimacy of lovemaking.

The wish-list trap starts in our childhood. There's a great parenting lesson here for us all to learn. Many children grow up learning that they can pretty much have whatever they want. Their parents never tell them no, and if they do, the children have only to beg long enough and eventually their parents will acquiesce. It's important to make "no" mean "no," so that children grow up learning that the world around them does not exist solely to give them all their desires.

Children who grow up never hearing "no" will find it difficult to focus on making another person happy. All their lives they have focused on themselves. They think, "I will force you to prove that you really love me. I'm not happy yet because you haven't done or purchased that special thing yet!" Reorienting their thinking at this point will be very difficult.

The Adults Around Us Have an Impact

The people around us, at work or even at church, can be part of the trap that promotes dissatisfaction. If, for a second, a spouse looks outside the marriage to evaluate the relationship, she will only become more dissatisfied. "Look how wonderfully Jeff treats Susan." That wife, looking at what she perceives to be a wonderful marriage, is only setting herself up to roll farther down into the valley of marital dissatisfaction.

Bill bought a new car and he was ecstatic about it. It was just the car he wanted ... until he listened to Ed. When Ed described all that his own new car did, Bill had to make a conscious choice: "Will I stay happy with what I have and what I was happy with before Ed opened his big mouth, or will I allow myself to become dissatisfied?" The decision to be content and happy must constantly be guarded. One moment I can be holding happiness in my grasp, and the next moment something or somebody can be trying to pull it from my grasp.

Allan was constantly trying to get his wife to do "just this one thing more and I'll be happy!" Yet nothing ever seemed to be that "one thing more." He never seemed to find the ecstasy he expected. Once he had finally coerced his wife into doing the latest thing on his wish list, he found that the next time they were making love, it was old and not as exciting anymore. That scared him. He would see something on a video or in a magazine and want to try it. Or he would hear someone talk about something and want to try it. A battle followed to push his wife just a little bit farther.

He very aptly and graphically described his situation using the word *ejaculation.* "I thought that it was the actual sexual ejaculation that I was in pursuit of. But I have finally realized that coercing my wife to do something that is just a little more out of her comfort zone has become the ejaculation. I've got everything backwards. I'm finding pleasure in pushing my wife away from comfort, rather than bringing her comfort. All this time I've been in pursuit of a 'false ejaculation'!"

Where Do We Begin?

Begin with the understanding that most people have a sexual wish list. "I just feel like he shouldn't want to do anything other than make love with me," one wife said in frustration. "Obviously I'm the wrong person for him if he doesn't just love me for me!" Not so! Everyone, even this woman, has a wish list. Once you accept that, look at your list with a critical eye. Evaluate each item based on the question, What is best for my marriage?

What Was the Plan?

God is not only the creator of the marriage relationship, he is also the creator of our sexuality. He has a plan for how we should relate to each other. He has a plan for how we should submit to and sacrifice for each other. Ultimately, his perfect plan is for our sexual relationship to be the expression of our love for each other.

For example, God does not want me to dominate another person. When I am called to love my neighbor as myself, I must start with my closest neighbor, my spouse. We are to serve each other.

God would not have you ask your spouse to do something that your spouse feels is morally wrong. Nor would he have you hold something over your spouse's head as if your happiness depends on what he or she will give in to. Threatening each other is immature behavior.

Is the list that I carry in my mind something that God would approve of, or is it a list of sexual fantasies that will only make my spouse feel less adequate? Holding the list up for God's inspection is certainly the first test. Remember, God created the sexual relationship. Some readers may have a hard time asking God to look at anything having to do with their sexual happiness. They see him as a very prudish, "no fun god."

Nothing could be farther from the truth. His very obvious plan was for each person, male and female, to find tremendous sexual pleasure as husband and wife. If that were not a fact, why else would he have created a woman's body with a clitoris? There is no purpose for a clitoris but sexual pleasure.

He made each of us in such a way as to find fulfillment and joy in each other's arms. Sexual wish lists can cause us to do just the opposite. A wish list that is demeaning or unending or scripturally unacceptable only makes a spouse feel unworthy and unacceptable. Nothing could be farther from God's plan and purpose.

"But looking at sexually explicit videos helps me get in the mood," one husband interrupted. "It's not hurting anybody! What could be wrong with that?"

Watching explicit videos disrupts intimacy by bringing another person into the "bedroom" of the mind. Focusing sexually on the body of a person who is not my spouse can only foster a lack of contentment with my own marriage relationship. It will teach me to start looking at others and make my spouse feel as if she, alone, cannot make me happy.

God's plan is not for us to unleash any sexual thought that comes our way. His plan for us is to find great intimacy and sexual happiness and ecstasy in marriage. But the plan won't work unless we follow his directions. If we don't, we can easily become addicted to chasing the excitement and miss the real intimacy.

It Doesn't Matter Why My Spouse Objects

When an area of a couple's sex life becomes an issue of dispute, a question needs to be answered: Why does my spouse feel uncomfortable doing this particular thing? Some spouses may or may not be able to give a logical reason for the objection. But whether or not the response seems to make sense is not the point. A spouse's willingness to listen to and accept the objection is very significant. Accepting the opinion is even more important than understanding it. A spouse should not have to exhibit keen debating skills to have his or her feelings or opinions accepted.

"What hurt me the most," one wife whispered through her tears, "was when you asked me why I didn't want to do that. When I tried to tell you how I felt about it, all you said was, 'That's the most ridiculous thing I've ever heard.' Then I knew that you were going to try to get your way regardless of my feelings. That's when we lost the intimacy!"

Forget the List

If you are motivated by your sexual wish list, try looking at yourself rather than your spouse. Your list probably indicates that you believe it is your spouse's responsibility to make you happy. In fact, your expectations are distressing both of you. You have allowed outside influences to define your sexual happiness in marriage. Leave the list behind! It will never bring you contentment.

If the List Threatens You, Draw the Line

A spouse who is dealing with a husband or wife who has an insatiable appetite to try things that are objectionable needs to decide where to draw the line. Darlene's husband wanted her to dress in such a way that she would turn on other men. He said it turned him on to take her out in public and have her display her body by dressing suggestively. She knew that was wrong, so she drew a line and told him she would not do that.

The line will vary from marriage to marriage. Some issues are non-negotiable, yet a spouse may continue to push for something that is morally wrong just because she wants it. Other issues, such as various sexual positions, are wonderful for some couples and not for others. These questions must be answered couple by couple. There is no universal answer.

A red flag should go up when a list gets in the way of intimacy or is unreasonable. Obviously, in these cases, the point has been missed. The sexual relationship was meant to pull a husband and a wife together, not to build a wall between them. When a wish list causes conflict in the marriage, it's time to rip up the list for the sake of the intimacy. It's time to grow up.

Summary

1. The belief that the items on a sexual wish list will bring happiness is a myth.
2. The sexual wish list is a never ending list that can replace sexual intimacy as the goal.
3. Sexual wish lists often come from outside elements in our society. They also come from the way many people in our culture were parented.
4. We need to develop a plan for dealing with the sexual wish lists in our marriages.

Making Sense of the Sexual Puzzle

1. What are the areas of your sex life that you argue about the most?

2. When you argue, is it your intent to win the argument and get what you want and think is fair, or do you want to find the answers to this conflict so that you can become more intimate?

3. When you look at these areas of sexual conflict in your marriage, do you really understand what your spouse is trying to tell you? Could you restate it from your spouse's perspective?

4. Are you willing to give up your perspective or wish list for the sake of the intimacy in your marriage? How can you demonstrate that willingness?

CHAPTER 8

Good-bye Passion, Good-bye Love

Rosemary's youngest brother, Peyton, came to our Thanksgiving celebration this year. He's a pastor in the Tampa area and has his own ideas about how to do things. Not only does he have his own ideas, but he gets very passionate about them. He is the kind of man who goes off into the mountains for an annual retreat. Now I go off to the mountains each year too. But I stay in a nice cabin. Well, actually it's a beautiful five-bedroom mountain home we borrow from a friend for a few weeks each summer. The roughest thing I have to do is figure out the computerized air-conditioning system.

That's not what Peyton means by "going to the mountains." He travels the mountain on foot, by himself, for a week, fasting and reading his Bible. It's a very passionate experience for him.

I didn't realize what having Peyton and his family for Thanksgiving would mean. When he pulled up in front of our house and got out of his four-wheel-drive vehicle (no normal car for him, of course), out came his own Weber charcoal grill and special hickory chips. Little did I know that this was only the beginning of a very serious tradition. To Peyton, the cooking of the Thanksgiving turkey was no joking matter. He was actually going to smoke it on his grill. What a weirdo!

Rosemary thought this whole event was going to be an exciting experience. I, on the other hand, liked to plan the completion of the turkey around the great football games. But Peyton had no idea when the turkey would be done. To this junior Eddie Bauer the cooking of the bird was not a process to be rushed or timed. When it was done, it was done. Instead of using a timer and a perfectly set oven, he stood over his grill and stuck a thermometer into the bird every fifteen minutes or so.

Five hours later, two-and-a-half hours late, the turkey was finally done! German that I am, this lack of scheduling was driving me crazy. But the passion with which Peyton took on the whole event added a tremendous amount of excitement. No sitting in an easy chair watching the game and waiting for the oven to buzz for him! He stood over his grill and nursed the whole project along.

Everyone claimed that this was the best turkey they had ever eaten. Who knows whether it actually tasted better or we just thought it did, thanks to the passion of the process. All I know is I found myself nominating Peyton as our Thanksgiving turkey cooker for life. No more ovens for us. What passion is there in a timer buzzer?

The Process of Passion Building

Passion is an extremely volatile, very powerful emotion in life. This emotion has caused nations to go to war. It has turned the tide of major sporting events and sent people out of movie theaters weeping. In the lovemaking relationship of marriage, passion is the excitement that takes over when exhaustion indicates that there isn't energy left to make love.

Passion is desire. Passion motivates us to block out every other thought and even reason.

Passion in lovemaking says, "I have this incredible desire to be intimate with you tonight. I don't want to hide it or act nonchalant about it." This open statement is naked and obvious, and it makes a person vulnerable to rejection and pain.

"Nothing makes me feel more like I've been slapped in the face," Diana began, "than when we start relating to each other in a passionate way and Trent throws water on the fire. Then he wonders why I'm not in the mood three hours later."

"What do you mean by 'slapped in the face?'" Trent, married only sixteen months, wanted to know. "How did I throw water on the fire?"

Diana told of a situation that had become typical in their young marriage. Several nights ago, she and Trent sat at the kitchen table for almost an hour after they had finished eating, and they talked. Then they took their coffee into their tiny living room and sat on the couch together. It was great. After talking and even sitting with his arm around her for a while, they kissed a few times and talked a little more. Just as Diana was about to pull Trent down on the couch, he very sweetly said, "It's almost 9:00. Do you mind if I watch the Raiders game?"

Diana said, "Oh sure, that's okay. I've got some homework to grade." So Trent gave her a kiss and walked off to the television set thinking, " I'm so lucky to have such an understanding wife. I'm able to put off making love until after the game tonight."

However, two and a half hours later, after the game, Trent walked into the bedroom to find a different scene than he had anticipated. Diana was in her footed pajamas, curled up, sound asleep. The picture all but said, "Don't you dare touch me!"

Earlier that night, Diana's mouth might have said, "Oh sure, that's okay," but her heart was crushed. They had been kindling passion that evening. Then Trent threw water on the fire. By choosing football over making love, he quenched the passion and injured Diana's ego. But Trent didn't know all that because he didn't understand the process of building passion.

Two Kinds of Fire, Two Kinds of Passion

We had spent all Saturday afternoon finishing our chores so we could take a break and cook out on the grill. No sooner did we get the hot dogs ready than it started to rain. Everyone was instantly depressed.

"I can't believe it," our youngest started in. "How could it be so beautiful while we worked, and then turn into a storm when it's time to play?"

"No problem!" I announced. "We'll cook the hot dogs in the fireplace!" With that announcement I headed into the garage to get some kindling and a couple of logs. My starting a fire in our fireplace is always an occasion for great laughter in our family. For some reason I have the hardest time getting a fire going and keeping it going. This was going to be a lot different from starting the gas grill.

I understand nothing of the principle of stacking the wood, placing the kindling, and drawing air circulation (I should never have dropped out of Boy Scouts).

Thirty minutes later I finally had a roaring fire going in the fireplace, and the house was half filled with smoke. No matter. We were hungry and ready to eat. Finally, after we had all finished bending over the hot fireplace cooking our hot dogs on the ends of coat hangers, we sat down to eat (all the while complaining about getting our faces scorched by the flame and about our imminent deaths from the coat hanger enamel that was probably melting onto our hot dogs).

As we sat there our daughter Torrey said, "This was great. We should cook them like this all the time." We all laughed. Each of us also knew she was right. Taking the time to do it that way added a lot of excitement to the whole event. Pushing an igniter switch on a gas grill and then sitting down to wait for the grill to preheat was easy, but it can leave you very uninvolved in the process.

Trent didn't know how wonderful that "fireplace passion" could be. Nor did he realize that he had already started the kindling. Diana felt that she had made her desires obvious. She had become emotionally naked and vulnerable to being rejected. Passion is like that. Trent had no idea that Diana was seeing his "relating" as an expression of passion. "What do you mean I rejected your passion. I didn't even touch you that evening," Trent said, proving his lack of ability to identify her kind of passion.

"Oh yes you did, but not the way you think," Diana began to explain. "You had your arm around me while we were talking on the couch. Trent, you think it was supposed to turn me on passionately when you finally came to bed and began touching my breasts. That may have turned you on, but it certainly didn't turn me on. In fact, it only made me madder. It isn't something that's just turned on and off like a switch. For me passion doesn't start with a sexual touch. It starts with a normal touch and a relationship."

Without realizing it, Trent had thrown a bucket of water into the fireplace. Though he may have wanted to light the passion again only a few hours later, it takes a long time for wet wood to relight.

Generally speaking, Trent and Diana are very typical. Women usually respond to the building, fireplace-type passion and men have that quick igniter switch passion. She builds toward a very passionate lovemaking experience. He, on the other hand, can turn it on and off as easily as closing the lid to the grill and turning the switch. This tremendous difference can be very frustrating if one spouse doesn't take the time to understand the other spouse's form of passion. It is frustrating enough to make each spouse hesitant to risk being so vulnerable with the other. Frustrating enough to keep the wood wet all the time.

Passion takes time. It's a building process. It's a kindling of wood that slowly ignites into a fire. When does the fire actually start to burn? It's hard to say. It's hard to pick the exact moment when the kindling stops and the fire is roaring. They seem to blend into each other.

There are several types of passion that can be present in a marriage.

Instant Passion

"You make it sound so difficult," a husband announced. "But it seems so natural to some people." When questioned about who his "some people" were, he thought for a moment and said, "I guess I'm talking about couples on television. They seem to get so worked up so quickly and effortlessly. Passion seems to come so naturally to them."

Passion is a very important, and necessary, part of marital love, but it's not the chemistry that we see portrayed on most television or movie screens. The instant passion they portray seems very intoxicating. But the reason it looks so inviting is because instant passion isn't a part of the real, long-term relationships of life. We do experience instant lust. But that's not passion, that's just lust. Movies portray two people who meet for the first time, and three minutes and a commercial later they are passionately ripping each other's clothes off. Again, that's both unrealistic and uncontrolled. It's giving in to lust.

"Do you mean to say that I shouldn't lust after my wife?" the same man asked. Certainly we should focus our sexual desires on our spouses. But there seem to be two very different kinds of lust. One is a covetous lust, a strong desire for something that I don't and shouldn't have, but I want anyway. If I think about the object of my lust long enough, I rationalize that it's okay to want it and then ultimately to actually have it. That's how people end up purchasing cars and other things that they don't really need or can't afford. A covetous lust is also how people end up justifying extramarital affairs.

The second kind of lust is the healthy relational lust. These desires are under control and focused in one direction. They are no longer self-centered. This is the lust that a person should have for a spouse. It is accompanied by the desire to see to it that the spouse is also pleased by the experience. Covetous lust is a desire that leads to taking what I shouldn't have, but relational lust is a desire for something that I already have and the desire to share the experience. Covetous lust is unfocused and undisciplined. Healthy relational lust is very focused and disciplined. It enhances the relationship and leads to marital passion.

Honeymoon Passion

"It's all changed, though," a distraught husband said. "We didn't have to work or 'focus,' as you call it, when we first got married. But it doesn't seem to come naturally anymore. If we lose the passion for each other, haven't we lost the love?"

He really wanted to get back on track. He wanted answers so he could make the right decisions before he either walked away from his wife or resigned himself to a dull marriage.

Another man was less distraught than he was sad. "There was no passion left between us," he said of his previous wife. "After about two years of marriage the passion just seemed to move out. So I moved on. There was another woman at the office that I seemed to have feelings for. Now I've found passion in my new relationship." When the passion was no longer automatic, this man walked out on his family and found a girlfriend to move in with. It wouldn't be long until he came back saying the same thing. "After about a year with my girlfriend, the passion left so I . . ."

Honeymoon passion should not be confused with real relational passion. Honeymoon passion is still self-centered and immature. The prevailing thought is, My new spouse will meet my needs. Specifically, she is looking for this new marriage to meet her relationship needs, which include sex. He is looking for this new marriage partner to meet his sexual needs. In honeymoon passion he views passion as very physical and sexual. In honeymoon passion she views passion as relational, ending with a sexual expression. After a while the relational gets dropped off and she can feel left out and used.

Trent and Diana had finally reached the end of this honeymoon passion stage. But that didn't mean they didn't love each other anymore. It meant that their marriage had progressed to a point where they needed to draw on their love to move to the next stage of passion, a more mature stage of passion. This is a progression that every marriage needs to go through. Once each couple passes through the honeymoon passion stage they begin having sexual conflicts. But these conflicts are only signals that should tell them the honeymoon is over and it's time to get down to a more realistic and more exciting form of passion. Not a passion that looks to take, but a passion that wants to share.

Relational Passion

Every marriage needs to move from the honeymoon passion to the relational passion. Relational passion is a focused passion that must be disciplined in two ways.

1. Don't Tempt Yourself

The demise of the honeymoon stage leaves a person very vulnerable. Vulnerable to glancing around with a covetous lust at other people. The discipline at this point is to bring those gazes home. At this stage each person needs to understand the driving force that unbridled passion can be. It's a decision of personal discipline not to look lustfully at anyone other than your spouse.

Sound silly? One friend even said, "It's okay to look, just as long as I don't touch." That's what an alcoholic thinks when he goes once more into the bar. "I'm not going to drink. I'm just going to be here and watch other people drink. I'll have a soda." It doesn't work. Why waste energy and thoughts lusting after something that I shouldn't be thinking about, when I could focus that attention on my spouse?

Dotti's was a story that we have heard in the counseling room over and over. She was a young wife who never intended to be unfaithful, but a guy at work was so attentive to her that she got hooked. What harm could come from having lunch together? It was so nice to talk to him. Before she knew it she was in bed talking to him. "I never dreamed this could possibly happen to me!" Dotti wept in the counseling room. "How could I allow myself to become so vulnerable?"

Focus the passion. Decide to be disciplined about it. Understand that its power can be very hard to resist and it can easily cause years of pain.

2. Meet Your Spouse's Needs

The second aspect of relational passion is perspective. Just as honeymoon passion was self-centered, relational passion is other-centered. A person with this perspective asks, "As we head into this passionate scene, what would my spouse enjoy?" Relational passion takes into account the needs of the other spouse. The issue is not whether one spouse understands or identifies with those needs. The issue is how to meet them.

In the ultimate form of relational passion you get turned on by the action of arousing the excitement level of your spouse as well as yourself. It's not foreplay. It's the excitement or intensity behind the foreplay. It's obviously not a "get." The perspective is that it's something you give and enjoy.

Passion You Decide to Build

The honeymoon passion is a bonfire that ignites in the early months or years of the marriage. But it is a fire that can be left untended. During those early years each spouse keeps coming back to the fire to take from the heat. But when neither tends to the flame, eventually it burns out.

When children are young they only want to put the foods that they know they like on their plates. As they grow older they learn to put foods from all the food groups on their plates. Relational passion is like a plate with several different foods. Some foods are enjoyed by one person and some by the other. The plate needs to have both foods because the spouses are sharing the plate.

Mature, relational passion must have relationship builders as well as sexually exciting events. He might not understand that getting excited about a walk on the beach stimulates passion, but she does. She may feel uncomfortable about getting undressed in front of him, but this ignites his passion. The plate needs to include food for both people sharing the plate.

This kind of passion is something that each spouse works on. Sometimes one spouse may be more attentive to the flame than the other. That's okay and natural for only a short period. But that situation should not be allowed to go for too long. The sexual relationship and the passion are both too exciting to let the flame go untended by one partner for very long. If this happens, one spouse must help the other to realize that they are allowing other things to interfere with the growth of their passion.

"It seems to be very close to foreplay," one spouse announced. It is very close. Foreplay is the actual action taken, but passion is the attitude connected with the action. Passion is the emotion behind the action. It's difficult to separate it from the action because some actions are actually outbursts of the emotion. Actions without the emotion, however, are passionless. If we neglect passion, we may begin to take our sexual relationship for granted and go through the motions without focusing and becoming excited.

Sometimes You Even Schedule Passion

Sometimes the fire is untended simply because one or both spouses are too busy. "What do you mean, I'm not very passionate anymore? I guess it's because we hardly see each other when we are both able to keep our eyes open."

Couples must decide to allow enough time to read about their marriage and then talk. They need time to make love rather than just have sex. Before marriage, they saw to it that they had time for each other. They scheduled dates so they wouldn't miss out on spending time together. Passion is often something that must be scheduled into a busy lifestyle. Scheduling passion means to allow for enough time to have a relationship rather than just jump into bed and have sex. That means a spouse needs to find out what his or her partner considers a passionate evening. If we are going to schedule it, we have to know what it is we're scheduling.

For some couples that may mean a night on the porch or in front of the fire just talking (with the television off). I just asked Rosemary what she would consider a passionate Saturday night event. It's December and she answered that question with a whole scenario. A passionate Saturday night event for her was to get dressed up, go out to dinner, then to the performance of the Messiah. That could not happen if it wasn't scheduled. In fact, very few things can happen in this busy life if they aren't planned ahead of time.

"Does that mean that we can never have a 'quickie'?" a man at a seminar blurted out before he realized what he was saying. He was referring to the fun of just making love without all the trappings of passion. Of course, that's often fun. But a couple cannot live by "quickies" alone. It's not just the goal that is prized. That's for honeymoon passion. After a while the whole process becomes the prize.

What About Those Who Are Guarded About Passion?

Passion is an emotionally naked thing. Some spouses find it difficult to be passionately open and vulnerable. Some would have us believe that those who are the most guarded about passion, those who find it the most difficult to be openly passionate, would be the conservative "religious right." Nothing could be further from the truth. A University of Chicago study of American sexual practices indicates that the conservative religious right may be the most uninhibited about their passion and sexuality.[1]

More than likely, the difficulty one spouse has with the display of passion may be the result of a non-nurturing relationship. That might refer to the current marital relationship or a childhood difficulty. Often when one spouse finds it difficult to overtly get involved in passion, it could be a sign of feeling unworthy. One husband summed it up well when he said to his wife, "It's real hard to act romantic or passionate when you've spent the whole weekend telling me how fat I'm getting. That doesn't make me feel as if I could possibly have a romantic bone in my body. In fact, it makes me feel like you might even throw up if I get passionate, undisciplined fat tub that I seem to be!"

Passion is a risk that must be nurtured a little at a time. Especially with a spouse who feels like he or she is not very passionate to begin with. The reluctant spouse is hesitant for a reason. A spouse must be made to feel adored. It's hard to feel passionate and romantic in comparison with the actors on television. For some it takes a tremendous amount of reassurance that they are not competing with anyone. They must feel loved and desired for who they are, period.

It Is the Process

Peyton was passionate about the entire process of Thanksgiving dinner, from cooking the bird to eating it. He didn't separate the process from the results. Not me. "If all you want to do is eat turkey," he told me, "why don't you just go to the Holiday Inn and order a turkey dinner?"

He was right. I didn't know that I really wanted the whole experience too. I actually wanted to be passionate about the whole process. In fact, the passion itself was part of the process. Even if we didn't get to eat the bird, the process itself would have been exciting.

Summary

1. Passion is the intense emotion and desire that surround the lovemaking.
2. There are two kinds of passion. Honeymoon passion is the strong desire to meet my own needs by taking from the sexual experience. Relational passion is the strong desire to find pleasure by meeting both our needs together.
3. Honeymoon passion is connected with the newness of the relationship. It very quickly runs out of steam. Relational passion needs to be built and maintained. It can be the passion that will carry a mature marriage for a lifetime.
4. Passion is a powerful force that needs to be acknowledged and disciplined.

Making Sense of the Sexual Puzzle

1. What kind of passion do I bring to this marriage, honey-moon passion or relational passion?
2. What kind of passion does my spouse project?
3. What form of passion does my spouse enjoy the most?
4. In what area of passion could our marriage use the most help?

CHAPTER 9

Myth: Couples Are Born Compatible

We were wrapping up a discussion on marital relations on the radio program "Family Time" when a woman called with this question: "My fiancé and I have been dating for over a year and we have stayed true to our commitments to be virgins until our wedding night. But what if we get married and find out we're not sexually compatible? What will we do then?"

This question has its roots in the last half of the 1960s. The "free love" thinking of that era was tremendously damaging to marriages. Young people were often encouraged to experiment with cohabitation before they made the decision to get married. Research has shown just how successful a predictor this practice has turned out to be. Those who live together before they marry actually have a higher divorce rate than those who do not live together before they marry.[1] Research also indicates that those who live together before marriage demonstrate a much weaker bond to each other than do those who marry prior to living together.[2]

Much of the argument for living together for a while to see how well they fit together seems to be based on the myth of general compatibility, which we would define as two people living together harmoniously—being like-minded in the important issues of life.

The idea was to test this "general compatibility" in every aspect of married life, including the sexual relationship. That experiment to test for compatibility didn't work, nor did it prove anything other than how immature all that thinking was to begin with. Generally, there is no *perfect* compatibility with another person, neither relationally nor sexually. But the less compatible we are, the more work needs to be invested in the relationship.

We Are Fooled for a While

Every time there is a job opening at Sheridan House, we fall into the same trap. Recently we began interviewing people for a new position, and one of the men we were talking to seemed to fit well. As a matter of fact, he seemed perfect. The more we interviewed him, the more we began eliminating all his competitors for the job. Finally, we made the decision to hire this particular man since his résumé fit what we were looking for. He seemed so compatible that hiring him would save us a significant amount of adjustment time.

When he started working with us we didn't take the time to work at getting to know him because we didn't think we were going to have to learn to be compatible with him. Eventually we began to run into problems because he seemed so different from the rest of the staff in so many areas. We weren't automatically compatible, and that shocked us.

The same process takes place when it comes to sex in marriage. At first the sexual relationship of the marriage seems wonderful. Passion and excitement camouflage the personal differences. For some, the conflict, or incompatibility, becomes immediately apparent. For others there will be a sexual honeymoon period. Then, after a while, the numerous incompatibilities surface.

"It just turns me off the way he's always grabbing at my body," Deena said to the counselor, in front of her husband.

"It didn't used to turn you off," Michael, her husband, responded. "In fact, it used to turn you on. Now nothing turns you on."

As far as Michael was concerned, his wife was never interested in making love. As far as Deena was concerned, sex was all Michael ever thought about. After they finished explaining to the counselor just how sexually incompatible they obviously were, their counselor said to their great surprise, "Well, that sounds pretty normal to me."

Their reaction was predictable. They were shocked to hear the counselor saying to them that this was actually the way it was supposed to be. They were supposed to be different from each other in their sexual expression. It was natural. The genders *are* incompatible.

One of the numerous results of the 1994 sexual research project from the University of Chicago was a statistic on the variance between the amount of time husbands and wives think about sex. Fifty-four percent of the men in this large national survey said they think about sex every day. Compare that with the fact that sixty-seven percent of the women said they think about sex somewhere between a "few times a week to a few times a month."[3] Once again, there's a great discrepancy here.

This is just a reference to the frequency and desire factor. It doesn't even consider all the other sexual incompatibilities that have to be dealt with. Before we even get to the different ways couples may think about their sexual relationship, we have to consider the fact that most of the time she's not thinking about it at all. The great valley of incompatibility starts before the lovemaking even commences.

It's just a fact. We are incompatible and we need to admit it and move on from there. Until we do that, until we admit it's not *just us* who seem to have a sexual incompatibility problem, we'll never realize that we're supposed to move on. We have to get past the myth that when two people get married, if they are a "perfect match," they will be automatically compatible in the bedroom.

The Myth of Sexual Compatibility

Most of the sexual relationships that we see on TV are either instantaneously passionate or totally dysfunctional. Many of the dysfunctional television marriages use their pathetic sexual relationship as a point of humor. When areas of sexual incompatibility arise, couples make fun of it and/or each other. We seldom see actors portray a couple working at making the necessary sexual adjustments. Either their sexual relationship appears to be great, or it appears to be horrible. The key word here is *appears*.

There is one marriage that some of us *have* watched develop—our parents' marriage. Yet the sexual aspect of their marriage is generally hidden from the children, since the details should rightly be left behind closed doors. Children, then, grow up learning about sex, thinking that their parents have one of three kinds of sexual relationship.

Some children grow up seeing the by-product of a great sexual relationship. Parents who wisely model a healthy marriage allow their children to see them being physically affectionate and romantic.

Other children grow up never having seen romance or affection between their parents. They grow up thinking that their mother and father have no sexual relationship at all.

Unfortunately, there's a third scenario. Some children grow up seeing their parents go through horrible, even abusive, sexual encounters. In fact, the child may be a recipient of the abuse. In the sexually abusive home, a child can grow up with a very warped perspective about sex in marriage.

All of these experiences have one thing in common: Children do not get to see their parents work through their sexual incompatibilities. The young married adult often moves into marriage with the assumption that either you are compatible or you're not, and that's all there is to it.

Nothing could be further from the truth. The fact that two people are either sexually compatible or they aren't is a myth. People might get married hoping they are going to be sexually compatible, but it won't happen. In fact, it is our belief that a husband and a wife are not even supposed to be sexually compatible. It could be part of God's creative plan for husbands and wives to start their marriages sexually excited about each other, but in reality, sexually incompatible.

We're Incompatible, Now What?

"What will we do if we discover we're incompatible after we're married?" the woman on the radio program asked. Couples married a decade or more have to deal with the same question.

What does a couple do when they come to the end of the honeymoon stage and find out that each one approaches the sexual part of their relationship very differently? What will they do when they realize that they are sexually incompatible? There are three options.

1. Ignore It

For a husband and wife to ignore the fact that they are different in their expectations and orientation toward sex is to say,

"Well, that's just the way we are and that's what we're stuck with. There is nothing we can do about it, so we'll just have to live with it."

That's a very sad approach, but it's also the approach that many marriages seem to take. At a seminar several years ago a man said to us, "My wife and I have wasted twenty-three years of marriage only because I didn't think we could change. I just thought that my wife was incompatible with me sexually and we had to live with it. When I heard you and your wife talk and I heard how similar we are to the two of you, I realized that you obviously had to make a lot of personal adjustments to each other. If you did it, why couldn't we? I only wish it hadn't taken me more than two decades to figure this out. Look at all the time we've wasted."

Some people tend to settle in their minds that they are incompatible and they're stuck with it for life. You're *not* stuck with it for life. There's action that you can take, but tragically, some people take the wrong action.

2. Find a New Partner

"After six years of marriage," a distraught man said, "it seemed apparent that we weren't compatible. She just seemed to lose interest in our sexual relationship, and my interest seemed to be getting more pronounced. It just wasn't working, so I left her. Now only two and a half years into a second marriage, the same thing has happened again. Once again, I'm in a marriage where we aren't compatible. I must not know how to pick them."

How sad, how arrogant. This man thought that he should be able to pick a wife who could better bend to meet his needs. He was picking a wife like he would buy a car. He wasn't willing to see that it wasn't a new wife he needed, it was a whole new attitude. When he discovered the reality that he and his wife were incompatible, he thought it was time to change partners. He bought the myth that there would be somebody out there who was perfectly matched and compatible with him. He missed out on the privilege of following God's plan and conforming to the needs of the marriage. That would have forced the personal growth he desperately needed.

3. Do Something Positive

When a couple comes to the realization that they seem to be incompatible sexually, they need to decide to do whatever is necessary to grow toward compatibility. It's healthy to realize and acknowledge that you and your spouse are not totally compatible sexually. Willingness to work at overcoming differences is a mark of maturity.

Overcoming Incompatibility

There are three very basic steps to take in overcoming incompatibility in the sexual aspect of the marriage. The process can be broken down into three "Ls": leave, listen, and learn. These three steps toward sexual compatibility require an initial attitude change that can permeate the whole marriage.

1. Leave Adolescence

The potential for pleasure from the sexual relationship is so great that each spouse is prone to want to take what he or she wants and hope the other person is happy with the outcome. That attitude doesn't work for very long.

Leaving adolescence means that a person is mature enough to decide to make the happiness of the one he loves a priority. In other words, a person makes a sacrificial decision to delay his own happiness for the sake of his spouse.

Adolescents characteristically want what they want, regardless of the consequences. A friend of mine asked me about how my daughter Torrey was doing with learning to drive. His daughter was at the same stage of life and they were having problems getting her to practice. "Lindsey firmly believes that when she turns sixteen I should flip her the car keys," my friend explained. "After the novelty of having a learner's permit wore off, she didn't want to spend the time practicing to drive anymore. She just figures that she should be able to drive wherever she wants the minute she turns sixteen."

This frustrated father listed the adjustments that his daughter was unwilling to make in her life. Lindsey believed firmly in her right to be happy—by which she meant that the family needed to get out of her way and give her the car.

"It does sound like a very adolescent attitude," I commented. "And there's no room on the highway for self-centered adolescents." When Lindsey is ready to make the proper adjustments and willing to act maturely, then she might be ready to drive.

Likewise, a marriage partner with an adolescent attitude is going to have a tremendous problem adjusting to marriage. That person will expect everyone else to adjust and give in. At some point each person needs to say, "I need to stop being self-centered. I need to look at our sexual relationship from the perspective of my spouse. How can I make my spouse happy?"

2. Listen to Your Spouse

Couples need to take time to talk to each other about their sexual relationship. For many couples, that kind of communication might be difficult, so they need help. A book like this one can help with the conversation about your sex life. Read a chapter out loud, stop, and talk. Discuss areas where you agree with the book as well as those where you don't. You may find yourself saying, "That part of the book really doesn't describe how I feel. This is how I feel." Let the book stimulate conversation.

Spouses are often hesitant to hit areas of sexual incompatibility head on. Perhaps she doesn't like it when she feels he is "pawing" at her before they make love. He doesn't really understand what she means by that, and they have discussed it on many occasions. But perhaps they never really listened to each other.

He may not have really listened to the depth of her feelings about the way he was touching her. "Oh, she really doesn't mean it. She's just in one of her moods." Then on the other hand, she may not have really heard that he was saying, "I don't understand what you mean." People have a hard time saying that they don't understand something, especially concerning their sexual relationship. Each of them needs to hear what the other person is saying, guarded as their declarations might be.

The only way to make my spouse happy is to decide to listen to what she is saying. The first time I went deep-sea fishing, I was with a friend who was an expert. He wasn't just taking me out in his boat; he had decided that he was going to teach me from start to finish. After we got to our destination, he stopped for a while so he could teach me how to tie the live bait onto the hook. The live bait was already bigger than any fish I had ever caught, so I watched him do it while he talked to me. Notice I said that *I* watched him while *he* talked. I wasn't really listening, because I just wanted to fish. I really didn't want a lesson.

Without listening, each spouse totally misses an opportunity to change and to help the other person. Without really listening, they only become more frustrated. Sometimes one hears the other talking, but doesn't listen to what is being said beneath the words. Adolescents just glare and refuse to listen, wanting only to be heard. Adults decide to listen, so they can make the proper adjustments.

3. Learn from Your Spouse

Two people need to face each other and adopt an attitude that says, "I'm willing to be less self-centered, and I'm willing to listen." People who agree to learn are agreeing to take a step toward their spouse's happiness; they want to learn how to make them happy.

The best way to learn is to try to do the things that a spouse says. Then give each other feedback. Just before Bob walked out of the door one morning headed for an early flight, he gave me a hug and kissed me good-bye in an especially warm way. It meant so much to me because I so often complain that the only time he seemed interested in hugging me like that is when he is interested in sex.

Later, I realized that I had never expressed to him how his hug—with no strings attached—had made me feel. When he returned from his trip, I needed to give him feedback.

I said, "I'm sorry I didn't say anything that night when you called from the hotel. When you hugged me like that, and we both knew that you were heading out the door rather than up to the bedroom, it made me feel loved for *me* and not for sex. Actually, it turned me on, and I couldn't wait for you to get home."

Learn from listening, and then make the necessary adjustments. But always ask for feedback. Ideally a couple will get close enough that they will eventually be able to give each other the much needed feedback before it's requested. Feedback about foreplay or things that take place during intercourse are very significant. Imagine how many people make love all their married life and never know that their spouse is turned off by something they do during the experience. Sadder yet is the couple that talks about it, but one spouse is unwilling to make the adjustments, unwilling to leave adolescence and learn.

Husbands and wives were created sexually incompatible. That's why we're not supposed to marry until we leave the adolescent stage of life. Unfortunately, it is this very area of the marriage that forces many couples to decide whether they are ready to grow up and become adults.

How Incompatibility Helps Us Grow

In 1964 I was sixteen years old and my family moved from Long Island to the Washington, D.C., area. I was miserable. I missed all my friends from New York, and I didn't seem to fit in with the new peer culture that was already established in my new school. I remember begging my father to send me back to live with friends in New York. This new group of kids seemed like they were just too different. It was too much of an adjustment.

My dad sat me down one night and said something that I didn't want to hear or believe at the time, but it turned out to be sage wisdom. "Bobby," my dad said, "this is an important opportunity for you to learn how to fit into a new group of friends. You are in the next stage of your life and it's time to grow. It would be easy for you to go back to the way you were on Long Island and not have to make new friends. But all through life, you're going to have to learn how to make adjustments and new friends. I'm not sending you back. We want you here with us, and we want to help you make the adjustment."

At the time I hated that whole conversation. But as an adult, I've looked back on those years of adjustment, and I now realize those were some of my greatest years of growth. I wasn't initially *compatible* with my new friends and this new, very preppy, community. But I eventually decided that, since I was here, I might as well make the best of it. As I made the necessary adjustments to their different way of dressing and looking at things, I eventually grew to realize that I liked it. Making these adjustments also helped me grow into deeper relationships than I had ever had in the past. As I learned to become more compatible, I grew personally. This was a great learning and maturing process for me.

Sexual Incompatibility Is the Catalyst

A wife sat in my office and begged for an answer. "Why do my husband and I look so differently at our sex life? It causes problems in our whole marriage. We could just go on through life and never have any arguments at all if it weren't for the fact that we can't seem to agree about making love."

Talking to this wife about her marriage made it very clear that this couple really didn't have a relationship at all. When she said that their sex life was messing up their relationship, she really meant that they were basically just a married couple going on through life with their own careers. They rarely talked about anything. Their sex life was the only area that was actually showing them that they needed to work on their whole marriage.

Although they don't really know each other like they think they do, a couple is usually very interested in a dynamic, fulfilling sexual relationship. The sex drive is like a magnet drawing a husband and a wife together. The sexual relationship, with its incompatibilities, should be a very significant and compelling reason for spouses to sit down and talk. It's a great relationship magnet.

Jim Talley says it so well when he says the husband has to learn to give relationship to get sex, and the wife has to learn to give sex to get a relationship.[4] We all have to decide to listen and learn so that we can love and give toward a great sex life and a wonderful marriage.

Summary

1. Shortly after the marriage most spouses come to the realization that they are not sexually compatible.
2. No one is perfectly sexually compatible.
3. Sexual compatibility is a destination that every marriage needs to seek. Arriving there takes a willingness to leave

adolescence, listen to your spouse, and learn about his or her likes and dislikes.

4. The strong desire that we each have for a fulfilling sexual relationship in our marriages makes sexual incompatibility the perfect catalyst for pulling the whole relationship together. Since both a husband and wife desire a better sexual relationship, they need to talk and listen to each other.

Making Sense of the Sexual Puzzle

1. When we make love, I like it when you _____.
2. When we make love, I don't like it when you _____.
3. It turns me off when you _____ in the hours before we make love.
4. It turns me on when you _____ in the hours before we make love.

PART TWO

Complications to Lovemaking

CHAPTER 10

Love in the Time of Children

D o you two have any kids?" came the rather sarcastic comment during the question time of the seminar. "I hear what you're saying, but I wonder whether you live the same life that we do? What do you do about your kids?"

Children can be a definite fly in the ointment of a couple's sex life. So many unexpected extras arrive with children that the sex life can be put on hold without the couple even realizing it. Before a couple knows it, it has been several weeks since they've made love. Actually, one spouse will usually be fully aware of the amount of time it has been. His biological clock is ticking.

Pregnancy

The first evidence of the need for sexual adjustment usually comes with the announcement that there's a baby on the way. Spouses have to work through their own different responses to the pregnancy and to the other person.

"When she told me that she was pregnant, a whole stream of thoughts came flooding into my mind," Jack announced to the new-parent support group. "Could we really afford a third person in our family? How would her attitude toward me change? How would her appearance change? Would I no longer be the priority to her? I had all these horribly self-centered thoughts that I couldn't possibly share with Sally. I felt I couldn't talk to her about them because she was so excited and my thoughts were so immature.

"Then it hit me," Jack continued. "One night while I was sitting on the couch, I finally realized that I was also about to go through a tremendous transition. I was taking on the responsibility of being a father. The finances, the change in our marriage relationship, and the thought of having the responsibility of raising a child . . . all this scared me to death."

Jack went on to talk about how this pregnancy was forcing him to deal with more adult issues than he ever had before. In effect, he was saying that up to now playing house was fun. Now the real adult life was about to begin, and he felt he had no one to talk to about it.

"I felt horrible saying anything to Sally about all my fears. After all, she's the one whose body is changing. She's the one who's going through the morning sickness. She's the one who's pregnant. How could I talk to her about all my concerns? And then there was the ultimate fear that I never wanted to verbalize, What if there's something wrong with the baby? It was just easier to avoid sitting down and talking. That way, these conversations wouldn't come up. We were used to talking together every night, but now I found myself avoiding it at all costs."

Sally had her own set of difficulties. She was going through the biggest transition of her life, and she was excited and anxious to talk about it. She wanted to talk to her best friend, Jack, about it, but he was acting funny around her. She really didn't feel much like making love because she felt like she was on the verge of getting sick most of the time, but she did feel like being intimate. But Jack was becoming more and more distant.

Sally's first thought was that she must repulse him, since her body was changing. If he didn't want to sit around and talk like they used to, it must be because he was turned off by her pregnant body. To make light of the whole situation, Jack even made fun of the "blimp" that lived in his house. However, his cracks about "wide load" signs brought tears instead of laughter.

Jack was only trying to bring humor to the situation, but Sally was devastated. This was supposed to be one of the most beautiful times of her life, and all Jack could do was make fun of her body and stay away from her. She wanted to be held, and he wanted to run from the whole responsibility. Each was reading the other's signals incorrectly. Jack wasn't sure how to handle himself, let alone his wife and their sex life. Was it over for nine months? Would she break something if they tried to make love? Why was she so emotional? Was she as scared as he was?

Opening the Lines

Unfortunately, many couples miss out on the opportunity to share the pregnancy experience with each other. Oh, they may go to the classes and share the birthing experience, but they don't share the emotional experience. Jack and Sally had to finally get to the point where they decided to talk.

Jack was very frustrated over the lack of sex in their marriage. Part of him felt guilty about his frustration. After all, she was carrying his baby. Every time he would give some kind of message about making love, he'd couple it with a "big" comment that would totally turn Sally off. He thought she was turning him down. She thought she was turning him off. Finally they reached a point where they exploded into conversation.

As they calmed down and actually listened to each other, they both learned a great deal about what the other person was feeling at that point. They may not have been able to identify with what the other person was dealing with, but at least Jack and Sally were now learning about it. At least now they were getting rid of their misconceptions. Each of them had felt abandoned. Jack was embarrassed to admit that the baby wasn't even born yet and he was already jealous of the baby-mother relationship.

Jack found out how his comments made his wife feel even more unattractive and less wanted sexually. By telling his "big" jokes, he was his own worst enemy. Sally talked about how she felt a little self-conscious about her new body anyway, and when he made fun of her, it made it impossible to get undressed in front of him, let alone feel desired by him.

Jack went on to admit that he wasn't even sure if it was okay for them to be making love while she was pregnant. He wondered if it could hurt the baby. If they could make love, how would they do it? He could hardly even stand next to her and kiss her anymore.

As they talked, they realized that they had both been making a lot of incorrect assumptions. They had both been misreading each other. Yes, they did need to be more sensitive to each other and these changing times. Yes, they did need to be careful about the things they were saying. Yes, they did need to talk more often and make sure they were both hearing the other person's fears and needs. The big yes was, yes, they could make love. In fact it just might be even more exciting as they experimented with the proper position to allow for most comfort. None of these "yes" answers would have come if they hadn't decided to talk about it. Jack and Sally could have missed out on a great emotional friendship during this special season of their lives. They also could have totally missed out on their sex life, if they hadn't decided to talk.

Demands of Infants and Toddlers

There is probably no greater time of exhaustion than the early years of parenting. These are the years when children are the most helpless and consequently the most demanding. Mom is always exhausted and Dad can't understand why she is so tired. Whether she works out of the home and picks the children up, or whether she works with the children in the home and trains them all day, mothering can be a thankless and overwhelming job.

The end of the day, when the kids are bathed and finally in bed, can be a time of great sexual stress. He's thinking, "Now it's my turn to have her." But she's thinking, "Now it's my turn to have me!" He has been waiting all evening for her, and she has no energy left for him.

This can also be a time of games and very poor communication. Rebecca sat in the counselor's office and made some very revealing confessions. "I knew that I should ask him to help me with the kids at night, but I was tired of asking. He knew I needed help, and all he did was sit there while I did everything. I found myself retaliating in a very quiet way. I stopped getting dressed for him. Instead I'd look as matronly as I could. I think I even stopped working at getting my body back, just to keep him away from me, literally." Rebecca's marriage was in deep trouble.

Rebecca's first step was to ask for help. She was doing the couple a disservice by assuming that her husband was deliberately not helping. It's not fair to make that assumption. The first step needs to be communicating the need for help. "I'd like to have a little time together this evening. Would you help me with the baths and the bedtime so we can have our own time?"

The division of parental duties is not only important for the sake of the marriage but also for the sake of the parenting relationship. In these early years, the area of discipline in particular produces stress and exhaustion. Many young mothers find themselves absolutely exhausted because they haven't thought through a plan for dealing with the toddler's rebellious behavior. The toddler comes with a "job description" that mandates pushing all the limits. Parents who set no limits raise a child who is more stressful to deal with. A toddler can also repel an inexperienced father from wanting to take on the parenting tasks.

A parenting and disciplinary plan greatly affects the health of the marriage. It's hard for a husband and wife to feel romantically inclined toward each other after they have just spent an evening arguing about a toddler's behavior and how to handle it. No one trained us to be parents. It has been said that we spend more time preparing to get a driver's license than we do to get a marriage license. Husbands and wives need to take on the task of parenting as a learning experience, together. Parents of newborns should be reading parenting books together to help them establish a parenting plan.[1]

Can't I Even Go to the Bathroom by Myself?

There's really a second step to the ongoing evening ordeal. Many moms never get a moment of silence during the day. Whether they work at home or out of the home, they are constantly on the go for other people. After asking for help with getting the children to bed, another statement needs to be made: "I'm going to take an hour to get myself together. Then let's sit out on the porch."

I remember asking Rosemary what she was going to do for that hour. Once she just wanted to take a bath without a toddler trying to get her attention. Another time she just wanted to take a short nap. It was a time for her to do whatever she wanted.

Mothers, and fathers for that matter, of toddlers have no way of knowing just how much their lives and exhaustion levels are going to be tested and what effect that testing will have on their romantic life. I often laugh when I hear new parents say, "We just had our first baby, and we're not going to let it slow us down at all." Very unrealistic and idealistic. A baby is supposed to change our lives, and we will need to make adjustments, but a child should not take control of our lives. We need to establish with the toddler "who's in charge here." That message will follow us not only into our bedrooms but also into the school age and teen years as well.

One of the first tests of this pursuit of who's in charge is very symbolic. It actually includes the marriage bed. The first test might come from the child who acts as if he or she must sleep with Mommy and Daddy. Every child would want to be a part of that fun slumber party. There are many parents who miss seeing the harm in letting a child manipulate that situation.

Reclaim the master bed. Let the child see that she won't be allowed to take over her parents' bedroom. Help her understand that she will be alright, and that Mommy and Daddy will still be there in the morning. This separation is vital, but the privacy of the master bed is also important. A child must not be allowed to interfere with her parents' sexual relationship.

The Exhaustion Will Continue If You Don't Plan

How long should a couple postpone their sex life? Should they decide to put their sex life on hold because she's so exhausted during the pregnancy? During the toddler years, when they're both still exhausted, should they continue to postpone developing their sex life? Does it get any easier when the kids hit school age? It didn't get much easier for us. There were still so many demanding activities, like soccer games, piano lessons, and now youth group. The list seems endless!

So how long does a couple postpone working on their sex life? Will there ever be a convenient time? "I just don't have time to think about my sex life right now," said a woman whose marriage was heading for disaster. This is an area where a couple has to decide to make time. Time to get some rest, time to communicate, and time to plan out their lives, so that there is some time left for them to be together. Far too often, we've heard people say that they didn't have time to work on various areas of their marriage, and yet somehow they found the time to sneak in an affair. We have to make the time for things that are important. A couple's sex life, and the communication that goes with it, is important enough to make the time, while there's still time.

The school age years aren't going to be any different. A couple will still have to decide to listen to each other and work together toward finding time to be together. Don't wait until you can fit it in. Make it a priority!

When Your Kids Are Older

One of the biggest difficulties when the children are younger is that there never seems to be any money to spend on getting out of the house for a date. However, at least you can get them to bed and have the house to yourself.

When they're in high school things change dramatically. Teenagers are able to stay up as late as you do. "I finally got to the point where I could get some privacy in my bed when we got our youngest back into her own room," one frustrated wife and mother began. "Then we found our oldest daughter following us around until bedtime every night. She thought it was our job to entertain her before we all fell asleep."

Parents of teens need to have the courage and wisdom to retake some territory in their home. Guilt often gets in the way of this process. "I feel so bad when I tell Torrey that we need some time alone together," Rosemary would say to me. "She can't possibly understand, and she acts as if we're rejecting her when we hint that we need to be left alone for the rest of the evening."

That was the time when I found I needed to take over. We had two opportunities here. One opportunity was to do some parenting by teaching our daughter a lesson that she can draw from when she herself is married. She needs to learn that husbands and wives need some personal time. She needs to see how significant intimacy is, and she needs to learn to make time for it. What better way to teach this lesson than to demonstrate right in front of her this need for personal marriage time.

The second opportunity was for us to actually make time for ourselves. If we waited for some marriage time that would come along by itself, we'd have to wait until both our kids went off to college. It's not natural for them to want us to be left alone. They want to be the center of our attention; unless of course they have something better to do.

We decided that Tuesday night would be the night to deal with this issue. That Tuesday morning I told Torrey, "Honey, at 9:00 tonight Mom and I are going to take over the family room."

"What does that mean?"

"That means that you will need to go on up to your room and read, or find something else to do—but you can't come down into the family room or into our bedroom."

"But 9:00 is too early for me to have to go to bed," she complained.

"I didn't say that you had to go to bed. I said that from 9:00 on you were banished from the family room or our bedroom."

"So what will happen if I come into the family room after 9:00?"

"Torrey," I said in mock seriousness, "if you walk into the family room after 9:00 you'll find two naked bodies in front of the fireplace." Really, she set herself up for my answer.

"Oh. Oh, okay," Torrey gasped as she walked away from this discussion altogether. Fortunately, the next morning, Wednesday morning, is my traditional day to take Torrey out to breakfast. While we were at breakfast, I asked her, "What did you think about my telling you that you were banished from the family room last night?"

"At first I was mad that I couldn't be with you," she said. "But then later on I was upstairs talking to Abbey on the phone, and when I complained to her that you had banished me from the family room for the night—and the rest of the things you said— Abbey said, 'Your parents are so cute together. You're really lucky.' It didn't bother me after that. In fact, it made me laugh."

Spouses need their time alone together, and our teens need to see that we need our time alone together. Sometimes couples just sneak it in and miss the opportunity to teach, as well as to get some privacy. I'm convinced that children who are able to observe that their parents really love each other and want to be together are children who are much more secure in this divorce-prone society we live in. Spending announced time alone on a regular basis is better for the kids than giving them your every waking hour. You need it and they need to know about it. They too will have to figure out what marriage is all about. Banish them!

Unbalanced Parenting Makes for an Unbalanced Marriage

What does parenting have to do with a couple's sexual relationship? Not relating well when we are working together as parents makes it difficult to relate when we are alone. Even worse is the situation where two parents aren't relating at all when it comes to parenting. One parent throws up his or her hands and says, "That's it. I can't do anything more with these kids!" Then that parent dumps the whole burden of the parenting job and responsibility on the other parent. It makes it very hard for that "dumped on" parent to feel very romantically inclined toward the "dumping" parent.

I still remember the big report on Florida that my fifth-grade teacher assigned Mike and me. As long as Mike saw me working on the project, he never did anything. And when I asked him for help he just played around. When the project was done, and we got our grade, he wanted to walk home together and celebrate. I was fed up with him and didn't even want to be around him.

How we accept the big responsibilities of life affects the way we celebrate together. How we take on the parenting project together has an enormous impact on how a husband and wife relate to each other sexually. If they argue and fight about the way the other parent handles a situation, it will make it very difficult to want to respond to each other later. If the home is in an uproar, with kids out of control, the desire to make love later on in the evening won't be easily kindled. If a couple is not helping each other out with the parenting process, it will be hard for them to want to be together sexually later on. Parenting and how we work together on it has a great impact on our sex life.

Summary

1. Pregnancy should not stop your sex life, but it will if you don't talk to each other.
2. Infants and toddlers will cause exhaustion for a young couple. New parents need to expect it and decide to help each other get the necessary rest so that they can have some time together.

3. One of the biggest conflicts in marriage is the discipline issue. Spouses need to take on these issues together as a team or they may find that they're not sleeping together as a team.
4. Parents of teens can still retake their home and their private life. It's a great example for the children who will probably have to figure this whole thing out for themselves one day.

Making Sense of the Sexual Puzzle

1. How do I help my spouse when it comes to the children?
2. On what parenting issue do we most disagree?
3. When do I help make arrangements for my spouse to have his or her own personal time?
4. What would be the greatest thing I could do to help our parenting relationship?

CHAPTER 11

Affairs We Never Knew We Were Having

The year was 1979. I had been working as Executive Director of Sheridan House Family Ministries for five years. I liked saying and writing that title, *Executive Director*. It was something that I used to define myself. I was proud of it and my work schedule proved it. I was working an amazing number of hours. After all, if I didn't do it, who would?

A new adventure was about to begin in our lives and our marriage. After seven years of marriage, Rosemary was pregnant with our first child. We were excited, but we were also a little worried, because Rosemary developed toxemia at the beginning of her third trimester of the pregnancy.

Then in her seventh month she began having excruciating headaches and we rushed her to the hospital. One morning, while I was standing over her hospital bed, I watched my wife go into a seizure. I yelled for help and the moment they saw her, they removed me from the scene and rushed her into surgery. Moments later I found myself sitting with a very serious doctor as he explained the situation. "We are very concerned about your wife and the baby," he began to explain. "We have just given Rosemary a very strong sedative and we are prepping her for surgery. We're going to have to take the baby immediately. I want you to know that there is a strong possibility we could lose both the baby and your wife. Her blood pressure has shot up to . . ."

I didn't hear anything else he had to say. When he said that there was a strong possibility of losing Rosemary, all the other more technical details became a blur. The doctor continued talking and I signed papers, but my mind went numb.

The next thing I knew I was sitting alone in a surgical waiting room while they worked to save my wife and baby. During the first hour of waiting, two of my closest friends came from two different directions. First Mike arrived. Mike is a physician, so he sat with me for a moment and then scrambled to find out what was going on. A while later I heard a voice at the reception table outside the room say, "I need to get in to see Bob. I'm his pastor." I recognized that voice and knew it wasn't my pastor! It was Joe Helms, the minister of music at my church.

They let Joe in the room and he just sat down next to me, silent for the longest time. Then he said what initially seemed to me to be one of the strangest things I could imagine. Joe looked over at me and said, "Bob, is there anything God might be trying to teach you in this incident?"

Wow! What bedside manner! "That's it?" I thought. "That's all you came to say?"

After a moment of silence I began to think. Joe's question was right on target. My fear of losing Rosemary helped me realize that for the past seven years of our marriage, I had been having an extramarital affair. Not an affair with another woman, an affair with my job. My job had been more important than my marriage. Meeting the needs of my job had slowly worked its way up to top priority.

I heard the message. At that moment I made a vow to God. I promised him that if he gave me my wife back, I would never again let anything come between me and our marriage. I promised him that after my relationship to him, my relationship to my bride would be my top priority—no matter how worthy any other project seemed to be.

After a few days in intensive care, I was given Rosemary back. I was also given a wonderful baby girl named Torrey. God gave me another chance, and I haven't wasted it. For the first time, I realized that spouses can have affairs with priorities, not just with other people.

The Three-Legged Race

When something takes priority over the marriage relationship, the relationship will falter. Few things can illustrate this better than those comical old three-legged races people used to do at picnics. In a three-legged race, two people are tied together at one ankle. If they don't work together and force themselves to get synchronized, they'll never make it to the finish line. If they do work together, they have a much greater chance of success. But if one of them is focused somewhere else, they'll fall for sure.

In our marriage relationship we can quickly get out of sync when one spouse is focusing elsewhere. When one spouse decides to make something other than the marriage relationship his or her priority, not only is the relationship out of sync, but intimacy is impossible. How can a spouse feel safe at being truly intimate when he doesn't feel as if he is valuable enough to be a priority?

"It's not my fault," Danny said with his wife listening. "She's never home. And when she is, she's too tired to want to do anything but sleep. For her to say that we don't have a marriage anymore is laughable to me. Her career became the all-consuming priority of her life. As a joke we even began to refer to her company as her lover. She was too tired to talk, too tired to sit, and too tired to make love. After a while I just decided that she had chosen the job over me and the kids. Then all of a sudden she wants to know what happened? Give me a break! What happened was that she chose her career path over us three years ago, and we got tired of waiting."

The marriage is a very jealous "animal." Most jealousy is unhealthy, but marital jealousy that seeks to protect the relationship and keep it a priority is healthy. Without this priority, the relationship becomes one of maintenance. We maintain or do the things we must do, but we do them without any relationship involved. When two spouses must have sex, they do, but that isn't making love. It becomes a job of dividing up the laundry, the dishes, picking up the kids, and meeting each other's biological needs. Sooner or later, that kind of nonpriority relationship trips and falls. Just like the three-legged race, you can't keep running in the marriage without focusing on your partner, and making that focus the priority.

Nonsexual Affairs

There are many things that motivate a spouse to violate the marriage intimacy by getting involved in a nonsexual affair. People have affairs for reasons. The reasons can always be boiled down to one ugly word: *selfishness*. To be intimate with a spouse I must be selfless. I must be willing to seek my spouse's happiness. If I'm not willing to learn to do that, then I'm left with the prospect of pursuing another person's happiness: my own. Either I decide to seek the best for our relationship, or I look at my marriage only as an opportunity to make me happy. The selfless approach can lead to deeper and deeper intimacy. The selfish approach continually violates the intimacy, causing one person to withdraw to protect himself or herself from pain. Part of that withdrawal could lead to either shutting down sexually or just going through the sexual motions.

There are four things we can have "affairs" with that are just as damaging to the marriage as a sexual affair. They are money, power, purpose, and relationship.

Money

The biggest temptation today seems to be money. Many spouses find themselves doing everything in their power to make more and more money. They pursue the money priority, all the time saying that they are only doing it for the good of the family, "so that we can have the things we want." Husbands, and wives as well, find themselves in this affair with money.

Many times one spouse has said in the counseling room that they are only spending this amount of time at the office for the good of the family. Ultimately it was untrue. Often a working spouse, who claims to be working for the happiness of the other person, refuses to listen to the pleas of that other spouse to come home.

It was never so clear and so sad as when Carl asked his wife what she wanted for Christmas and Suzie said, "To be with you. All I want for Christmas is for the two of us to go away together." For Christmas this very affluent executive gave his wife a new Lincoln instead.

He was having an affair with making more money and with the things that money could bring him. The more money he made, the more intoxicated he became with it. But it never brought him all that he wanted, so he just pursued making more. He gained an empire and lost a family in the process. Making money became his mistress, yet he could never see it. His wife gave up and became very cold, but when he finally realized that he had abandoned her for the "money mistress," it was too late.

Power

There are things other than money that draw people out of the home in search of happiness. Many spouses lust for power. They abandon their homes in the evenings to serve on boards or committees. By leaving the marriage relationship, in which they have no idea how to find fulfillment, they hope to rediscover the excitement of activities that brought fulfillment in the past.

As one wife put it, "I'd been involved in a lot of activities in college, as chairman of several very glamorous committees. When I married Alan, he was involved in his professional life, while I was just beginning mine, and the glamour and power were gone. I felt like a nobody. In fact, I felt like Alan's life seemed very exciting. I know now that he was actually struggling for significance just as much as I was. That's when I think I began looking for an opportunity for a power base again. I knew how to find happiness and excitement working hard on short-term committee projects. I didn't know how to find happiness in a marriage. So I gravitated to what was easier, to take on projects rather than take on this relationship. To escape my failing marriage, I found myself diving deeper and deeper into the local Republican party work. There I was finding real power again."

This well-known wife found power in her committee projects, but she lost the intimacy in her marriage. Her husband was jealous of the time and priority that her party work was requiring. He had a choice to make. If she wouldn't listen to his requests for them to spend more time together, he could either dive further into his own profession or find someone else to spend time with.

Wouldn't you know it! This all blew up in her face two months before the biggest election of her volunteer career. To quit the party work at that time would probably mean never having an opportunity to get involved at this high level in the political process again. Couldn't her husband wait until after the election? He quickly reminded her that he had been waiting for four years. That realization was a shock to her. How could this intoxicating drive have been going on for that long?

Having extramarital affairs with power is very demanding. Power always promises that the next rendezvous will bring ecstasy, but these encounters are never fulfilling.

Purpose

The pursuit for power and the pursuit for purpose are often entangled. Some people search outside of their marriage in a quest for power, but others search for purpose. Either the marriage relationship has not brought them the power or purpose that they have sought or they don't know how to find it. Either reason is no excuse. Belonging to numerous activities outside the home that are taking away from the marriage relationship cannot be justified by frustration in the marriage itself.

"She won't leave her career and I can't understand it," a frustrated husband almost screamed. "We've waited all these years for this to be possible. In fact, I've worked for years to help make it possible. It was a goal we *both* established. Now with my income I'm doing more than well enough for both of us to live, and she won't quit her job. She acts like I'm asking her to divorce herself from that job she works at. I'm just asking her to do what we both used to want. I'm asking her to come home to me."

He described it perfectly. She initially went outside the marriage to find purpose and self-esteem. He was gone all the time establishing himself, and she worked to help them get started. But after awhile, without the marriage relationship to make her feel as if she had purpose, the office where she was working began to meet more than the need for money. Before they knew it, she was unwilling to get out of that "bed." Working at the office gave her purpose and a feeling of value she'd gotten used to. Would going back to the marriage relationship, in order to find purpose, do the same? It was a risk she was not initially willing to take.

Relationship

As we have stated previously, the root of a great sexual relationship in the marriage is a strong marital relationship to begin with. The blossoms of sexual intimacy on the tree of marriage are first watered through the roots of the relationship in general.

Many couples, especially in the early years of the marriage, miss out on that relationship because they become so busy doing other things. Then one day they find a great need for relationship. Why not? All through the time of dating they had a relationship with each other. Now, after a few months of marriage, the relationship has eroded.

People look in many places for relationship, and once they find it, many are reluctant to let go. They escape into relationships that may be fun or very important, but not as important as the marriage relationship. Some husbands search for that relationship in softball leagues. They sign up for every opportunity they can to play and be with the guys. Some wives develop that relationship around their children. They find themselves devoting every minute to the needs of the children.

There's nothing wrong with these activities in and of themselves. They become wrong only when they interfere with the marriage. It's not even the activity or job that is wrong, but rather a person's attitude toward the activity, job, or child. When anything other than the marriage relationship begins to take priority over the marriage, or even challenges it for first place, then it is damaging. As the previous illustrations demonstrated, whatever couples placed in a priority position above their marriage damaged the marriage commitment. Analyze your activities, careers, and even your relationships with your children. Have they reached a place of priority over your marriage?

Why Is It So Easy to Fall into These Affairs?

Everyone has a desire to be needed. Everyone has a need for gratification. Those needs were meant to be worked out and supplied by the marriage relationship, but two things interfere with that process. It takes a long time for a couple to work through the early difficulties of immaturity, to finally arrive at an intimate relationship in the marriage. In the process of working out these rough edges, feelings are often hurt, and people withdraw rather than move forward.

A second reason that might encourage people to look outside the marriage to find gratification is that we get married without having any idea how to work toward intimacy. "If marriage is sup-

posed to make me feel more complete and valuable," one wife
said, "somebody should tell my husband, because it sure hasn't
happened." We simply don't know how to work at becoming intimate. We understand the need for sex and the desire for a sexual
relationship, but we don't get married with an understanding
about how to blend those desires with the desires of a spouse.

Overcoming those early difficulties is often a very long
process. Many couples, or one spouse in a marriage, can choose
to skip the whole process. They feel that it's just too hard to feel
valuable and figure it all out. Many find it easier to look outside
the marriage to meet their needs.

The Violation Is Damaging

When one spouse is aware that the other spouse has a
stronger desire to do something outside the marriage, marital intimacy is violated. The violating spouse might not even be aware
of the fact that something has stepped in between them. "I
thought Ellie was being totally ridiculous when she said that I
liked to play softball more than I liked to be with her," one man
confided. "She even went so far as to say that I'd probably rather
play softball than make love with her. 'Just sleep with your softball glove,' she said to me one night. Then one evening, some of
the guys told me they were going to join an additional softball
league so they could play three nights a week. When I said to
them, 'Sounds great! Count me in!' I immediately realized Ellie
was right. I had a problem, and I needed to deal with it. I was
avoiding going home. I needed to go home where I belonged."

When a spouse finds that she is competing with something
else, anything else, it's got to shut down her desire for intimacy.
It shuts down that desire because she feels rejected. Being open
and vulnerable, or emotionally "naked," is difficult when a spouse
feels as if she isn't the priority in her spouse's heart. Affairs with
anything destroy the potential for an intimate relationship. Hence,
the sexual relationship will be damaged.

Focus and Refocus

Some couples may believe that they will never have an affair,
so they don't really feel as if they need to watch out for this kind

of marital interference. Other spouses have gone so far as to even announce that something else is more important than their marriage. Many pastors' wives will attest to that.

"We can't plan anything," one pastor's wife told the counselor. "As soon as we get ready to do something, his 'mistress' will beep him and he's gone."

"It's the church she's talking about," the pastor proudly explained to the counselor. "I'm a minister. I need to be available to my people. She just has to understand that."

This man was confusing his relationship to his Lord with his relationship to his calling. He was also suffering from a messianic complex: "Of course no one can take care of these difficult situations at church but me. That's why they call me," he reasoned. The pastor didn't realize that part of his calling was to set an example of how to be married according to God's plan. This husband and wife needed to commit to their marriage relationship without anything coming between them, even the congregation.

He needed to focus on the things in his life that he decided were important. He needed to open his calendar and look at how he spent his time. Did he spend any uninterrupted time working on his marriage? Was he able to say to other people, "No, I'm sorry I can't make it to that meeting, since my wife and I have already scheduled something that night"?

When we focus on how we have been, we will quickly find out that we need to refocus on how we should be. What schedules do I need to change? What activities do I need to remove from my life and schedule? What marital activities do we need to put into our calendars and lives?

We spent time with that pastor and his wife one weekend, while we were presenting a seminar in his church. After he heard what his wife was really saying, that she just wanted to feel like their marriage was a priority, he agreed to sit down and refocus on his schedule. When we returned the following year to present the next marriage seminar, he and I went out to lunch, while Rosemary went out with his wife. The pastor said some amazing things at that lunch.

"Since you left last year I've dealt with my 'mistress.' I now have a phone answering machine at home, so I can screen for emergencies. My wife and I are doing great in our personal life and spending scheduled time together each week. You know, our intimate relationship has gotten better also. As we have decided to make our marriage our priority, I feel like we've fallen in love again. Funny thing is, I feel like I'm doing a better job as a pastor now also. I guess I just needed to get my priorities in order." His wife told Rosemary exactly the same thing. She no longer felt like she was competing with a mistress, so she felt safe to express her love completely. All because they had refocused.

Another husband said it very succinctly: "I feel like my wife is having an affair with the church she attends. I know that sounds funny . . . and I feel guilty even saying it like that. But every waking moment she's over there, and I can't seem to get her home to even talk. I just can't compete with that 'suitor.'" When a spouse feels like he is competing with anything, it's only natural to withdraw sexually.

What is it that gets in the way of your marriage relationship? What are the potential attractions that draw you away from your marriage? We have mentioned only a few. As you focus on your relationship with your spouse, be alert to the power of the draw as well as the actual event or item.

Summary

1. Spouses often end up having extramarital affairs with things as well as people.
2. An affair is any person, place, or thing, including a career, that is placed in a higher position of priority than the marriage relationship.
3. Looking to meet unmet needs from their marriages, people fall into affairs with their careers, activities, or even their job of parenting.
4. Couples need to look at their schedules and priorities to see if they need to refocus their lives to save their marriages.

Making Sense of the Sexual Puzzle

1. What is the most important thing in my spouse's life?
2. What would my after-hours (when I'm not in my normal workday schedule) calendar indicate is my priority in life?
3. What areas of our lives are cutting into our marriage?
4. What do we need to cut back on?
5. What can we do as a couple that will help us re-establish our marriage as the priority relationship?

CHAPTER 12

The Intimacy Earthquake

Imagine that every day on your way to work, you drive your car over a bridge. The bridge spans a beautiful, lush valley with a winding stream banked by a rainbow of wildflowers. Many days you even leave your house early so you can stop for a few minutes and breathe in the beauty and tranquillity.

Then one day, just as you're driving over the bridge, there's an earthquake. The same bridge that you've enjoyed for years collapses, and your car is hanging over an edge. Crawling out of the window of your car, you escape just before the car plunges into the valley. Still inside the car are friends that you love. They are killed on impact.

Driving over that bridge used to fill you with feelings of peace and tranquillity. But now, even as you approach the ruined bridge, the beauty of the valley stands in contrast to the blackness of your grief and pain.

This illustration came from a man who used the bridge as a metaphor for his marriage. When he found that his wife was having an affair, his marriage, like the bridge, crumbled away.

Love and Respect

In Ephesians 5:33 Paul said: "Each one of you also must love his wife as he loves himself, and the wife must respect her husband." This passage beautifully describes the different kind of love that each spouse wants. A wife wants to feel cherished by her husband, while a husband dreams of feeling respected by his wife. Marital infidelity devastates both love and respect.

For Her

When a wife finds that her husband has had an affair, the relationship bridge collapses. For her, the affair says that their relationship wasn't worth protecting. It says that she was cherished so little that the intimacy that was rightfully hers was handed out to a stranger. The trust and security that she looked for in the relationship are gone.

A wife comes to the marriage to be cherished and protected. But an affair destroys her sense of security. The relationship that was supposed to protect her is now causing her excruciating pain. She no longer feels loved. "I never felt so naked and all alone as the day that I found out that Robert was having an affair," admitted Barbara.

For Him

A husband wants his wife to look up to him and respect him for who he is. The relationship should be a partnership where he feels valuable. Her respect should be a respite for him in a constantly competitive male world.

When a husband finds that his wife is involved in an extramarital affair, the entire balance of respect is destroyed. "I felt as if they must be meeting and laughing at me," a devastated husband reflected. "I know in my head that I was the last thing on their minds when they were together, but my heart pictured them saying, 'This time is for that loser, Ed!'" Ed's wife had given away his most valuable possession, the belief that she respected him as a husband.

Where Do We Go from Here?

Countless couples have sat in counselors' offices with their heads in their hands crying, "An affair has ravaged our marriage! Where do we go from here?" Unfortunately far too few have realized that they can rebuild that bridge of intimacy. Often spouses simply want to walk away when they learn that their partner has had an affair, even if their partner begs them not to terminate the marriage.

Rebuilding that bridge is extremely difficult, but it can be done. There will probably be moments of flashbacks and pain for years to come. But those flashbacks will come whether or not the marriage stays intact. "I thought that the moment I was granted the divorce, the pain would stop," one wife said. "But it didn't. I still imagined him with that other woman. I still had flashbacks of pain to endure."

The best initial plan is to make the decision to work through the devastation. It may be a very long time until intimacy is restored. Biological sex may be restored to the marriage in a moment of passion, but sexual intimacy will take significantly longer. Both the violating spouse and the violated spouse will need to heal. Unfortunately, as they heal, they will need to be helping each other heal. Two hurt people must try to mend each other. It's a difficult, but worthy task.

How Do You Know the Marriage Can Be Healed?

How can a couple possibly know that they are going to be able to be mature enough to allow the marriage to heal? By choosing to take action, a couple can move toward restoration. The initial load, however, will be on the shoulders of the violating spouse, the spouse who had the affair. The key word there is *had*. Repairing a bridge is impossible if the earthquake is still in progress. A marriage cannot begin healing if the affair is still going on.

1. Go Cold Turkey

The first step toward saving a marriage is for the violator to walk *completely* away from the affair and any further relationship with the person he or she was having the affair with. "Cold turkey," I remember a man saying. "You mean just like that, end the affair?" There is no other way to restore trust and love to the marriage than to walk away completely. The man asked that question in the counselor's office, and then went on to lie to his wife and say that the affair was over. He promised that he would never make contact with his mistress again. Only weeks later did his wife realize that her husband had lied. This lie and the continuation of the affair made the rehabilitation of the marriage even more difficult, if not impossible.

Severing all contact with the other party in the affair is the first indicator that a marriage can be put back together. Without this step, a couple may stay married but the sexual intimacy will never return.

2. Find a Mediator

The second step for many couples ravaged by infidelity would be to allow a third party to help them rebuild the bridge. It will be easier for many couples to practice driving back over that reconstructed bridge if they have a third party in the car with them for instruction and interpretation. Many couples will want to seek the help of a counselor as they work at overcoming the infidelity.

3. Turn Off the "VCR"

The third step is to decide not to make any video recordings of the affair. "Oh, that's ridiculous! Who would do that?" asked a husband whose wife had had an affair. The counselor had just asked him why he was making a video of this whole horrible event. The husband thought the comment was out of place. "Not so," said the counselor. "Every time you demand that your wife tell you all about the affair, you create a video in your head. Every time you push her to give you more details about the affair, you create a video that you will have to replay. Every time you act as if you deserve to know the information about the affair, you create flashbacks for yourself that will make it harder to overcome this whole devastation."

When a couple is trying to make it back from an affair, they should make a pact with each other that no details will be shared. The violated spouse won't ask, and even if he or she does, the violator won't give the details. It just lengthens the process of recovery. The details only make for a longer mental video tape that must be destroyed.

4. Take Some Risks

Focus on healing your spouse. The only way that intimacy is going to be restored to the marriage process is if each spouse risks walking out of their self-preservation, defensive mode. After a marital earthquake caused by infidelity, coming back out from behind the wall of emotional protection is very risky. But healing can't commence until one or both are willing to risk being hurt again.

"This is crazy," said a wife violated by her husband's affair. "It's just too risky for me to start working on this marriage again. It's too risky to trust him again. Why should I open myself up to the possibility of such pain?" She should open up for the potential of healing the marriage. The safer attitude might be to close up and refuse to risk. But the marriage will never heal as long as that is the posture taken.

The violator risks the possibility of never being forgiven. The partner who has been violated risks the possibility of being hurt again. Both risk the possibility of never being able to put the marriage relationship back together again. With that much at stake, both spouses must be willing to make a commitment to risk.

"It's just not fair," a man who had been violated blurted out. "I know that I love Barbara, and I want our marriage to work out. But part of me keeps screaming from the inside that it's just not fair. Why should I have to forgive and risk getting hurt again? Shouldn't I just sit back and make her prove herself? Shouldn't she feel some pain? Maybe if I went out now and had an affair, that would make us even. Just giving in and forgiving her doesn't seem fair."

He was right. It wasn't fair. But what is? *Fair* is a very adolescent word we use when we feel we haven't gotten our way in something. Life isn't fair. Joining the great adolescent crusade for *fair* is a waste of time. I need not focus on *fair*. I must focus on where to go with my life. Fair or not fair is not the important issue to debate. Rather the focus should be on what I will be glad I did several years from now. We will each be glad we did the best we could do to work on the marriage.

5. Get a New Perspective

Understand the healing process from the other person's perspective. Again, this may take the assistance of a counselor. In the process of healing, each spouse must understand the difficulties that the other spouse is going through. The goal is not the healing of an individual, but rather the healing of a relationship. Intimacy cannot be restored unless each spouse gains an understanding of the whole relationship.

When the Violator Isn't Receptive to Rebuilding

The steps that follow are predicated on the fact that the violator is repentant about the affair and wants to do whatever it takes to rebuild. If, however, the violating spouse is not interested in discontinuing the affair or in healing the marriage, these steps are irrelevant. The violated spouse can't go through these steps in the hope of winning the violator back from an affair. The violated spouse will need to step back, get help, and decide on a plan to make a last-ditch effort to show the violating spouse what he or she is about to walk away from. These might include drastic steps, and should not be done without wise counsel. *Love Must Be Tough*, by James Dobson, is a book that has been very helpful for many couples when dealing with this problem.

For further clarification it will be helpful to break down the roles of each spouse when an affair has devastated the marriage. Both the violator and the violated spouse have significant jobs to do in order to rebuild intimacy.

The Task of the Violating Spouse

The spouse who has been involved in the extramarital affair has a great deal of rebuilding to do. It will take tremendous focus. It will also necessitate tremendous patience and strength. One of the factors that led up to the affair might be the fact that the marital sex life was very poor. "We wouldn't have gotten to this point if she hadn't been so cold to me," one husband rationalized. "Now you tell me I need to wait even longer until we can be together. What if she's never ready to make love again?"

The point is not sex. The point is to focus on rehabilitating the marriage and relationship. The situation is like that of a farmer who ruined the soil by farming for short-term needs. He didn't think about the future of his farm. Instead he just worked the soil without putting anything back. Finally he hit a season where he had done so much damage that the soil wouldn't grow anything. The agricultural specialist came out, tested the soil, and said, "This soil is going to need a lot of investment of minerals and time."

"That's fine," said the farmer impatiently, "but when will I be able to plant a crop again?"

"Not for several seasons," the specialist responded.

"Not for several seasons!" exclaimed the farmer. "You've got to be kidding! How can I wait for several seasons?"

"I'm not the one who caused this problem," the specialist responded. "You caused it. Now you're going to have to work with it."

In answer to the husband who really wanted to know how long it would take until the relationship included sex, we say that it will take as long as it takes. That farmer was about to find out if he was really a farmer or just a harvester. In the same manner, that husband needed to find out whether he was a husband or just a taker.

1. Seek Forgiveness

The first step for the violating spouse is to ask for forgiveness. This forgiveness needs to be extended beyond just the spouse. It needs to include asking God for forgiveness. Forgiveness is nothing to be toyed with. A spouse who asks for forgiveness needs to demonstrate her sincerity by turning away from the affair and every behavior that surrounds the affair.

One wife involved in an affair stopped the sexual involvement, but still thought she could keep up a relationship with her former lover. "But I just need to call him and make sure he's okay." Any continued involvement will only slow down the process. As stated earlier in this chapter, asking for forgiveness means walking away from any contact.

2. Rebuild Trust

The spouse involved in an affair must decide to rebuild the trust. The violator must take steps that will place him beyond suspicion. "I knew that Rose wondered what I was doing after hours," a husband explained. "Because of my past involvement with another woman, I knew that she began to worry every evening when it got to be one minute past the time when I should be home from the office. I decided to relieve her of that worry by making sure I got home every evening before 5:30. That meant I didn't work any overtime. That meant I didn't get involved in any discussions past five. That meant I decided to get home immediately so that I wouldn't cause her any more unnecessary pain."

This wise husband said that he didn't initially like having to do that. Rose didn't ask him to do it, but he knew she worried. His pride often whispered to him, "You're a grown man. Why are you rushing home like a little boy?" He would fight that rebellious thought and say to himself that he was going home because he didn't want to do anything that would hurt his wife and stifle their growth.

Becoming trustworthy is a long process. It's not done because the violator is on probation. It's not even done because the violated spouse demands it. Readjusting one's life and schedule is done so that the violated spouse can work on feeling secure in the relationship again. Rose made an interesting comment: "I used to do fine until 5:30 every evening. Then every minute after 5:30 I would get more and more depressed. I would wonder if he was sitting somewhere with *her*, and then my mind would fantasize horrible things. Even though I was confident that these fantasies weren't true, I couldn't seem to stop. By the time he got home, I was a mess. When he made the decision to come straight home, he relieved me of a tremendous amount of pain and doubt. In fact, that step went a long way toward making me feel valuable and secure again."

The violating spouse should take any step possible to rebuild the trust. All the while, these steps should be taken with a posture of patience. He will have to be willing to work the field slowly, like the farmer, patiently allowing his spouse to heal before expecting progress in the marriage.

3. Redevelop the Relationship

The third step in this marital rehabilitation process is to develop the relationship, rather than dive into the sex life. Wait for the sexual relationship until the violated spouse is ready. In the meantime, decide to work on building the marital relationship. Read books on marriage and seek counseling. Decide to take advantage of every option available that will help the marriage grow. But all through this process the thread of patience must prevail. Grow the relationship by talking, listening, and learning, and be patient with some of the repeated flashbacks.

Fred wanted to know why his wife couldn't just get past this and move on. "Sure I did it, and I'm unbelievably sorry," he admitted, "but she needs to get past this thing." Fred didn't understand that time will be the strongest medication for healing. But it must be time in which the trust is not damaged in any way. In his impatience, Fred damaged his marriage further by placing a phone call to his ex-lover.

The Task of the Violated Spouse

The violated spouse must get to the point where he or she can live for a period of time without imagining his or her spouse with another person. That takes a desire to focus on future growth rather than on past mistakes. The violated spouse must decide to trust that God can get them through the devastation. This is a necessary daily process, and most of the focus needs to be on God rather than on the spouse. The violated spouse must learn to trust the healing power of Christ and the Holy Spirit, rather than succumb to the power of this affair to cause pain.

1. Determine to Forgive

The violated spouse must make a daily decision to forgive the violating spouse. Each day, when the doubts and the pain creep in, decide again to forgive. Forgiveness is not a feeling. If it were a feeling then we could only forgive if we felt like it. Forgiveness is a decision a person makes. In fact, even if the violating spouse never asks for forgiveness or comes back to the marriage, the spouse who has been violated must forgive. Without that step there can be no growth. Neither personal nor marital growth can take place without forgiveness. A very valuable book on the topic of forgiveness is John Neider's *Forgive and Love Again.*

2. Decide to Trust

Choosing to trust a mate who has completely breached the fortress of marital trust will not be easy. The wall may have to be rebuilt slowly, one brick at a time. As the violated spouse, don't feel that you are obligated to immediately grant full trust. You and your spouse may need to construct a step-by-step plan to reestablish marital trust. Determine what is most important to you. Do you really need him home at 5:30? Are Saturday mornings a difficult time? The two of you must communicate to establish reasonable boundaries. But it is up to the violated spouse to set the pace in granting trust.

However, please remember that relationship progress will only be delayed when one person tries to control another person. There will come a day when trust will have to take place. The sooner the better. Before one spouse smothers the other spouse.

A violated spouse who steps into the marital rehabilitation process trying to keep her spouse in solitary confinement will only end up imagining that her spouse is finding a way to cheat. If one spouse takes on the role of being a detective, eventually everything will start to look suspicious.

3. Resolve to Return

The third step for the spouse whose heart and marriage have been violated is to decide to step back into relationship. That means that the violated spouse must decide to love his spouse as if this infidelity hadn't happened. An attitude like that is next to impossible. It must be reestablished every day, perhaps every hour. When the pain or a flashback infects the heart and mind, the decision to love again, as if nothing has happened, will be dashed on the stones. That decision must be recommitted to over and over again.

This decision to love again means that the violated spouse will respond toward his spouse without condemnation, not with an attitude of, "I deserve this special treatment after what you've done to me." That "I deserve" attitude is not an act of love, it's vindictive.

The hardest part about loving again will be to risk intimacy of heart and body. For many who have been violated, making love will be difficult for quite a while. For many it should start by just holding each other until the day arrives when both spouses are comfortable with this final step of intimacy by interlocking their minds, hearts, and bodies in intercourse. Violated spouses should take their time, but they should also risk putting the relationship back together. All the while, they should bear in mind that their spouse is also hurting and looking for verification of forgiveness. For many marriages, a regular reminder of that forgiveness will be the vulnerable step of making love.

Each of these steps has included the word *decide*. None of these steps will come naturally. No one will automatically feel like forgiving a person who has caused so much pain. No one will naturally feel like trusting a person who has failed so dismally with that trust in the past. No one will automatically feel like loving a person who has betrayed him. The fact that these are not steps anyone would *feel* like doing automatically means that we must *decide* to do them. This will be a very hard decision to maintain without the power of Christ in a person's life. Only through Christ do we see that ultimate decision to love, when he said, "Father, forgive them . . ." as the soldiers finished nailing him to the cross.

In order to get past the pain and on with the rebuilding of the marriage, the violated spouse must decide to take steps. Not steps concerning what the other spouse should have to do, but steps toward forgiving, trusting and loving the other spouse.

Risk Intimacy

The final step for each spouse will be to risk intimacy when *both* spouses are willing to risk. Generally one will be overly anxious, while the other spouse will be fearful. The violated spouse might be fearful of what the other spouse is really thinking about while they are making love. One woman confessed, "I had to get past wondering every time we made love whether he was thinking about me or her." The violator must patiently reassure his spouse that he is only thinking of her.

Adjust Your Focus

A couple who risk making love again after infidelity will need to make two adjustments in perspective. First, they must focus on the process, not the product, and second, each must focus on the other.

Many times a spouse will be ready to be intimate but not ready for intercourse. The time spent being physically naked and holding and touching each other might be as far as she is able to go at first. If both spouses decide to focus on the process, then it will be okay, though perhaps frustrating, to stop with the nakedness and petting. This will also reassure the violated spouse that the other spouse is not in bed with a mixed motive. The violated spouse needs the reassurance that it is the relationship that is really the goal, not the relationship that is the manipulated vehicle to get to the sex. Focus on the process of the relationship rather than getting to the prize of the product. Remember the farmer who needed to learn to go for more than a harvest.

In addition, each spouse, violator and violated alike, must decide that when they make love, they will work at focusing on only one person, their spouse. Their focus should not even be on meeting their own needs. Instead of leaving their minds blank to the excitement and passion, they must determine ahead of time to focus on the happiness and excitement of their spouse. Focusing completely on one's spouse while making love will help determine that nothing else will creep into the mind. It will also help each spouse feel that his or her needs are a concern of the other spouse.

If spouses don't decide ahead of time to focus, they could easily allow their minds to wander. They could also very easily miss the signs that the other spouse is not able to continue at that time. If the message is missed, a spouse might continue to push forward and a battle will ensue. The event will end in disaster.

This whole experience of giving to the other person and focusing on the needs and limits of the other person is the essence of making love. Giving the experience to each other is important. For example, some violated spouses tend to use sex as a tool for power. This kind of retaliation is extremely destructive. Sex should never be withheld as a punishment or until the violator proves that he or she "deserves" sex again. It should always be freely given and received with sensitivity. It should be handled with the other person's heart and needs as the priority.

Each person will handle these needs differently, however. Each spouse will perceive responses differently. The process of the relationship, even the sexual relationship, must be read and listened to carefully so that the couple moves ahead together. Both spouses must take their time.

One wife summed up her feelings of trust in a very unusual and yet contemporary way. "This will sound strange," she began. "But when Arnold decided to go through the humiliation of being tested for AIDS before he made love to me, it meant a lot. I knew he was dying to make love, but he didn't want to do anything that could jeopardize my safety or the children's. The fact that he went back into our sexual relationship slowly and that he cared enough to get checked made me feel loved again."

Summary

1. When an extramarital affair has hit a marriage, steps can be taken to restore the intimacy.
2. These steps are most effective when both spouses want to restore the marriage.
3. The steps require risk and great patience.

Making Sense of the Sexual Puzzle

1. What are the steps that you can take to reassure your spouse that you are committed to this marriage?
2. What are the things you do that make your spouse feel insecure about the marriage?
3. How can you show that you are willing to risk putting the marriage back together?
4. How can you avoid ever being tempted to become involved in an extramarital affair?

CHAPTER 13

When She's Not Interested

Sid and Amy had been married for seven years, but after only two years of marriage, Amy lost all interest in sex. They rarely made love. At first it was a topic of constant discussion. Then it became a focal point of arguments, but neither of these approaches worked. They still made love only on rare occasions. These were the times when Amy felt like she "owed it to Sid to let him have sex with me," as she put it. Now they were at the point where their comments about their sex life were basically only sarcastic barbs.

Sid and Amy had pretty much accepted that their marriage would not include a sexual relationship. He was very frustrated and she felt very guilty, but they were both trying to live with this marital difficulty.

Then one night they were out to dinner with a couple they had been friends with for a long time. Their friends started talking about a marriage retreat they had attended where they had decided to rededicate their efforts to build a great marriage relationship. "Our sex life, which used to be nonexistent, has gotten much better," the wife said.

Sid and Amy often felt frustrated by comments from people returning from retreats and seminars talking as if the event had changed their lives forever. "It'll wear off," Sid thought. "Just give it a few weeks."

"When did you go to this life-changing seminar?" he asked flippantly.

"That was over a year ago," the other man responded. "But it wasn't the seminar that changed us. The seminar just got us started. We were the ones that made the changes in our marriage relationship. We started trying to understand each other. There's no comparison to the way our relationship is now and the way it used to be."

The rest of the dinner was very quiet. In the car, finally alone, Sid asked Amy, "Have you been talking to them about our marriage?"

Amy admitted that she had indicated to the wife that they wouldn't need separate bedrooms when they went on vacation with them, because they never did anything anymore anyway. "When I said that," she continued, "Sheila and I talked for a while about the fact that you and I don't really make love much."

"I suppose you told Sheila that it was my fault," Sid fired back.

"No." Amy looked down at the floor of the car. "I told her I thought there must be something wrong with me, that I just didn't want to have anything to do with sex. I told her that it wasn't you, it was me."

With that very tearful and transparent admission, Sid pulled his wife across the front seat, and they drove the rest of the way home silently, sitting closer than they had in years.

When they got home Amy said, "I don't want to be the way I am. I want to try to change my attitude toward sex. But I've been afraid to say that out loud because I'm afraid to give you the expectation that I can learn to enjoy making love. I just don't know where to begin."

The Road to Why

The husband seeking to understand his wife's loss of sexual interest must determine whether he is going to travel alone or with a guide. Ideally, a couple would be so willing to work on their sexual relationship that they would not only talk to each other, but they would also seek the assistance of a marriage counselor. "That would be so embarrassing," one person wanting help responded. Embarrassing or not, it's better than spending a lifetime wishing for help, but refusing it because of the opening five minutes of embarrassment with a counselor. Once the topic is placed on the table, in the counseling room, the counselor will then be able to help a couple get past the discomfort of talking about it, both with the counselor as well as with each other.

If one spouse is unwilling to go to a counselor, that's no reason to stop trying to work on the difficulty. Perhaps the next best answer is to bring the counselor home. Purchase books about the sexual relationship in marriage, such as *The Gift of Sex* by Cliff and Joyce Penner. These books offer the most help when they are read out loud, one chapter at a sitting, and then discussed. Using a book on the subject is the second best way to open the lines of communication on sex in marriage.

Many times a wife won't have any idea why she isn't interested in making love anymore. That can be very frustrating for a husband oriented toward problem solving. In this instance, the task is not one of solving a problem in one hour, but rather opening the lines of communication about the subject. A wife will need to feel safe in discussing this very emotional topic. She will need to feel as if it's okay if she doesn't know why. Safety in this discussion is more important than answers.

Her lack of sexual interest needs to be approached as if it's a marital problem rather than merely her problem. The focus needs to be on them rather than her. The primary job of the husband here is to listen and try to help his wife talk about the issues. It might even take great discipline on his part not to pass judgment or disagree with what she is saying. The only way to encourage her to press forward is to listen and be helpful rather than confrontational.

"I know she really believes what she is saying," a confused husband stated. "But it doesn't make a bit of sense to me. Why does she have a hard time making love because of something that was said two days ago or because we haven't finished painting the bedroom and the room is a mess? I just don't get it." But this wise husband knew that it didn't matter whether or not it made any sense to him. For too many years he told her those reasons were ridiculous, and for too many years she just clammed up and stayed away from talking altogether. This time he was learning to allow her to have her own opinion. He was going to listen without contradicting or butting in or offering the "insti-fix" solution. He was not only listening, he was also affirming. "I can't say that I totally understand your reasoning, but I do know that these things have an effect on our relationship. Somehow I have been wrong in not doing my part to take them more seriously."

Don't Drive Too Fast

Amy was dreading her first discussions with Sid. When he just looked her right in the eye and listened intently, however, she was greatly relieved. "No condemnation?" she thought. But the final and most powerful encouragement came at the end of the night when Sid *didn't* finish the conversation with, "Now, are we going to make love tonight?" He shocked her by kissing her good night and rolling over.

Months later, after tremendous progress, Amy even commented on that particular night. "You know what was one of the most wonderful things you did the first night we started talking about this?" Amy said to Sid. "It was when you didn't demand that I perform that night. It was when you didn't expect me to make love right away. I was dreading going to bed after that discussion. Then when we went to bed, all you did was kiss me good night and roll over. My heart was racing with fear and you calmed my fears by saying with your kiss, 'We don't have to make love. I know you're not ready to do more than talk right now.'"

Sid responded to her compliment about that night with, "That was one of the hardest things I've ever done. My head and heart kept telling me I needed to give you time. But my body kept saying roll back over and give it a try."

Then Sid and Amy did something they hadn't done in a long time. They actually started laughing about themselves. They laughed so hard that eventually they were crying. Finally Sid reached across the table, took Amy's hand, and said, "We're going to make it, aren't we? Look at us, we're even laughing about it."

It all started with a willingness to talk. Amy felt safe to start talking because Sid created a safe environment. There were no strings attached. He just listened and helped where he could. No judgments or blame!

But What If She Won't Talk?

Many husbands reading this might feel as if they may as well just give up, since their wives refuse to talk about the issue of their sexual relationship. But the first question to consider is why she won't talk. A husband may be able to answer that question by looking at the way they have talked about it in the past. Perhaps it has become a time of blame and judgment. Maybe the subject has become a battlefield with both sides intent on winning at all costs.

Once the reason for not talking has been explored, the next step is to change the approach. If she won't talk, that's still no reason to quit trying to work on the difficulty. Again, the fact that a couple's sex life has shut down needs to be approached as a marital problem, rather than just *her* problem. If the problem is approached as the responsibility of the couple, then the husband can work on his portion too.

The husband in this circumstance needs to step back and analyze what he may have done to push his wife away from an intimate relationship. Once he has thoughtfully examined his approach to his wife and their sexual relationship, he needs to make the necessary changes.

"I've done that," a husband is now thinking. "I changed my approach to her and it was a waste of time." *Time* is the important word here. It took years or even a lifetime for a wife to develop the attitude she has toward the sexual relationship in the marriage. Those attitudes aren't going to be changed overnight. It will take significant time for her to be willing to believe that the changes the husband has made are permanent. Only then will she consider risking a change of any kind.

For the husband who is going this road in a one-seater, don't give up. Instead, give attention to what you can do to improve your approach to your wife and the whole topic of sex. It may start with unconditional love and acceptance. But it will take time and patience.

What do you have to lose? You can either spend the next twenty years wishing you and your wife were relating, or you can decide to spend those years working on the problem. There's some consolation in knowing that you gave it everything you had.

Causes of Sexual Apathy
Previous Negative Experience

People view their sexual present and future through the glasses of the past. For many wives, especially, the beauty of the sexual experience has become distorted due to sexual abuse that took place in childhood or the teen years.[1] Professional help may be needed to deal with the past before the future can even be considered.

Many husbands have great difficulty figuring out why their wives are repelled by a sexual relationship in the marriage. "What have I done to cause her to be so turned off by sex?" is the silent question looming in that husband's heart. The answer for that husband is "Nothing." He may have done nothing to bring about his wife's sexual difficulties. The damage was done when she was a child.

Even though he didn't do anything to cause the damage, a husband can do a great deal to help repair it. Patience with his wife's difficulty and gentleness in handling the topic of sex are crucial. Then he can gently help steer her in the right direction to begin getting help to deal with the past trauma.

In other cases, a husband might have unknowingly contributed to his wife's disinterest in making love. For a woman, each pleasurable sexual experience causes her to desire the next sexual experience. But the contrary is also true. Each undesirable sexual experience with her husband causes her to become less interested in making love.

"For the first two years we were married," Rhonda confessed, "we, or should I say, he had sex with me and I never had an orgasm. In fact, I got to the point where I didn't even anticipate having an orgasm. When I didn't even think that I was going to be satisfied by the whole experience, I stopped trying to find satisfaction. Eventually the only thing I found myself trying to do was to avoid the situation altogether."

A husband, who approaches the sexual experience with such a strong biological drive, might not even be aware that his wife is not fulfilled. If he is aware that his wife is not finding pleasure in their sexual relationship, he might think that it is because something is wrong with her. Perhaps she wasn't really trying hard enough. That husband is not aware of the very significant part he plays in his wife's sexual happiness.

In the cases where a wife has lost interest in the couple's sex life due to a lack of fulfillment on her part, it is up to the husband to find a way to bring her happiness. He must be willing to ask questions and then listen to his wife. "You treat our sexual relationship as if it's just for you," a wife fired at her husband when he asked her why she seemed to avoid him sexually. He could have chosen to fire back or he could have chosen to stay calm and ask her to help him learn to do a better job of understanding her needs. Chances are that she doesn't understand them herself. That could be frustrating to a husband initially. "How can I help her if she doesn't know what help she wants, or if she even wants help at all?" They need to work together to discover and understand more about her.

Together they can learn what she finds arousing, as she tries to show him where to put his hands and how to touch her more gently. Together they can decide on the right place and atmosphere for making love. She can help him slow down so that she can get excited at her own pace. It may be a very slow process, but they can both learn together.

What about the husband who doesn't seem able to go at his wife's pace, the husband who has premature ejaculations? This can be a physiological phenomenon, and a physician can prescribe medication for it.[2] On the other hand, it might be a situation where the husband thinks he is focusing on his wife and trying to bring her pleasure, but really he is still focusing on his own arousal first. The discipline of focus could be a key here. This husband must attempt to focus totally on his wife and her needs, attempting, as difficult as that seems, to put his arousal aside. It will require a great deal of concentration on her, and she should not touch him in any way during this time to arouse him. The Penners have written about various techniques to deal with the problem of premature ejaculation.[3]

The past sexual experience of many wives has included the pressure to have an orgasm. Each time they made love in the early years of marriage, their husbands wanted to know if they had an orgasm, and if not, why not! Not understanding that her happiness is not *as* wrapped around an orgasm as his fulfillment is, he becomes very concerned about her not being able to "perform." The pressure to have an orgasm can get so great that it actually becomes very difficult to have this orgasm. Hence it's easier not to even try. When she didn't reach orgasm, he felt like a failure and made her feel like a failure. He simply didn't understand that she was different from him. Neither did he understand the pressure he was putting on her.

Another area that is very difficult for some couples to discuss is the experience of a former marriage. Many spouses who have been through divorce still have tremendous trauma lodged in their minds about the things that happened in the previous marriage. The pain, and the memory of that pain, is sometimes so great that they find it difficult to give themselves completely to their new marriage. Even though they looked forward to this marriage with great expectation, perhaps even seeing it as a rescue from the past pain, once in the new marriage, the flashbacks from the past make them very defensive about trusting completely again.

A woman in a second marriage takes the risk that her new husband will not perpetuate the pain from the past. No one comes into a second marriage without carrying considerable baggage, but that baggage must be left outside the door. True, she might be hurt again. But when she chose to get married, she chose to give herself completely to this husband. When she chose to get married she left herself with no options but to risk trusting.

Marital Self-Esteem

"It's hard for me to think about making love," Lonnie confessed. "It has nothing to do with Pete. It's all because of me. Ever since the baby, my body has changed. I don't feel attractive anymore. In fact, I feel like I'm a whale. I don't even like taking my clothes off."

Lonnie went on to say that she didn't feel loved or desired anymore. When her husband tried to protest and say that she was being ridiculous, she looked at him and said, "How long do you think it has been since you have told me that I turn you on when you look at me?" When he said he didn't know, she told him it had been over a year.

It only takes a couple of comments from a husband about his wife being overweight to get her to keep her clothes on. When she feels unloved or no longer attractive, she can also feel unworthy of seducing or participating sexually with her husband. "When his lack of attention makes me feel like he no longer finds me attractive, I would wonder what he was thinking about when he did see me naked. When we were making love I would wonder if he was really thinking about one of those cheerleaders he was staring at in the football game. It was too emotionally painful for me to even think about. To cope, I just avoided the situation."

If romantic gestures or loving words are a turn-on, rejection is the great turn-off. Many husbands don't even realize that they have been the ones to turn their wives off sexually. By placing career or leisure activities ahead of his wife's attempts at romance and togetherness, a husband silently communicates a strong message of rejection to his wife. She feels unable to compete with his colleagues or teammates. After a while the constant rejection becomes too difficult to bear. She simply gives up.

Can't Please Him

Many wives have lost their interest and desire for a sexual relationship in their marriage because they have been made to feel as if they will never be able to please their husband. He is constantly pushing for new and different sexual things for them to do. Once she does them there's always another experience. She slowly becomes aware of the fact that she is not turning her husband on. Instead, he focuses on his "wish list." His lack of desire for *her* needs becomes a turn-off. His lack of desire to enjoy himself in her and her alone is a turn-off. His self-centered attitude is very unromantic and childish. It too is a turn-off.

Turning herself off to their sexual relationship is a significant defense for her. She has been made to feel that she can't turn him on without doing the next strange thing he comes up with, so why risk thinking that she can? To protect her own self-esteem, it's just easier not to ever be the one who approaches him to make love. She assumes, from past experience, that he'll just try to push them into doing something they haven't done yet or watching something they haven't seen yet.

He Has an Inordinate Appetite

"Roger complains that I never initiate our sex life, but he never gives me a chance. He comes after me every night. I'm exhausted physically and emotionally. I get to the point where I feel like just getting it over with by servicing his needs. In fact, if I could avoid it altogether for a day or two or more, I might be more aggressive. He doesn't give me a chance."

Most men have a significantly greater sexual appetite than women.[4] Some husbands are so sexually driven that they don't give their wives a chance to think about whether or not they want to make love. Not giving his wife a break from their almost nightly sexual experience meant that Roger never gave his wife a chance to even think about it on her own. If she did think about it, she was thinking of ways to avoid it. Roger could greatly increase her desire by decreasing the amount of time he spends thinking about sex.

When questioned about the amount of time Roger spent thinking about sex, it became apparent that he was constantly doing things that were arousing: the kind of movies he watched before he went to bed, the kinds of magazines he read. Roger was becoming aroused by the fantasy of looking at other women, and then he wanted to meet this biological arousal need with his wife. He needed to take a serious look at his lifestyle patterns.

All men who think about making love to their wives every night are not as extreme as Roger. Some don't even think about sex until they see their wives getting undressed for bed. The suggestiveness and visual stimulation of getting undressed is all it takes. In these cases also, it would be important for a wife to understand that she is turning her husband on without meaning to. She might not be able to keep up with him if she is continually, yet unintentionally, arousing him. Couples can discuss this topic to help them better understand each other. If he wants her to be excited about their sexual relationship, he might have to give her space to get excited. If she thinks he's always aroused, she should make sure she's not giving the wrong signals. If she's not the one, they will want to look at what he's doing to get aroused nightly.

Too Busy

Many couples just don't have time to make love. They are so exhausted all the time that they just fall into bed. Here, however, we find a basic difference between the husband and the wife. I once heard it explained like this: A woman goes through life with one large battery that gives her energy. This battery gives her the energy to do all things. This battery energizes her to work, to relate, and to have sex with her spouse. When the battery is run down, she finds it difficult to want to do anything.

A man, on the other hand, has a battery that energizes everything he does, except sex. He can be totally exhausted, with this main battery run down to zero power. Then he gets into bed and a second little side pack battery kicks in! This little extra battery powers nothing but his sex drive. No matter how tired he may be, if the side pack gets triggered, he's in business.

Several years ago Rosemary and I were driving back from speaking at a conference that was several hours away from our home. We finished speaking at ten o'clock at night and decided that we'd drive until we were about to fall asleep, pull into a hotel, and then resume driving the next day. At one o'clock in the morning we pulled into a hotel, exhausted. When we reached our room, we began to undress for bed and I made a comment that was an invitation to make love.

"How could you have any energy left to even suggest that we make love?" Rosemary asked in bewilderment.

Something happens to me when I check into a hotel with my wife. No matter how tired I am, the newness of the hotel triggers my spare battery! I need to understand, however, that wives don't have one of those side packs!

We have already established throughout this book that a wife needs the foreplay of a relationship. If she's exhausted from working outside the home or from managing the home itself, it's difficult for her to find the energy to make love. If she has to become aroused without spending time in the relationship, she feels that she is missing something. For long-term sexual satisfaction the woman needs an emotional, intellectual relationship with her husband.

For the sake of the marriage, both spouses must reach back and find ways to come up with extra energy. He needs to find energy for relating, and she needs to find energy for making love. Busy people still find the time to have extramarital affairs. They find a way to get the rest. They find a way to have a relationship, and they find a way to engage in sex.

We need to acknowledge that we lead busy lives. Research indicates that our busy lifestyles will impact our marriages and even our sex lives. If we can't make significant changes in our lifestyles, and most of us can, then we need to find ways to get rest, so that we can continue working on our marriage. Many women are too busy to have the energy to make love. The question is, do they need to sacrifice some of the things in their schedule or their marriage? No one, no matter how competent they may appear, can have it all. Sacrifices must be made somewhere.

My Husband Turns Me Off

"He's gotten so heavy that it's hard for me to even think about wanting to make love. I've told him that he needs to lose weight if he wants me to get excited about making love, but it hasn't done any good. He diets for a while and then eats."

This wife believes that she is justified in having no interest in making love with her husband because he turns her off physically. She is acting as if she is putting a carrot out in front of him that will encourage him to lose weight "for his own good." Except this isn't for his good. It's just a further devastation to his self-esteem, which means that he will just eat more because he is depressed.

The fact that a husband might turn a wife off isn't his problem, it's *their* problem. When she indicates that he, in effect, repulses her, she dooms the marriage. If his goal in the marriage is to be respected, and she shows just how little she respects him, she is placing the marriage on very thin ice. This man may or may not lose weight. He may even lose weight because some other woman at the office thinks he's wonderful for who he is rather than because of how he looks. A man on a quest to feel worthy becomes very vulnerable to the attention and admiration of others if his marital self-esteem is low.

A better approach for this wife is to decide to love her husband beyond her feelings about his weight, just as she would want him to do for her. By doing this, she might build back his self-esteem. Turning him away only pushes him further into the

hole of low self-esteem. She's sending him back to the comfort of
his "mistress" called ice cream and cake. In this particular case,
the wife needs to be the one to initiate the response to her husband and to their sex life. She needs to love him unconditionally.
Her refusing to accept him fully until he makes some physical
changes is a powerful force that will drive a great wedge in the
marriage.

Physical Pain

Another possible reason for a wife to avoid the sexual relationship is physical pain. Some wives have indicated that they
experience great physical pain when making love. Friction caused
by a lack of adequate vaginal lubricant or one of a number of other
physiological reasons can make it painful to make love. The saddest thing about this is that some cases can be so easily remedied.

When physical pain is a problem during the lovemaking
experience, the wife should go to see her gynecologist. If the
gynecologist is unable to offer frank solutions, seek a second
opinion. Many of these physical difficulties are easily corrected.

"I could just cry," one wife lamented. "All those years I
avoided making love with Jim because of the pain, and after fifteen minutes of discussion, my doctor prescribed a lubricant.
That's it. These past months have been wonderful. I'm actually
looking forward to making love for the first time in our marriage.
It makes me sad to think I waited so long to talk to my doctor just
because I was embarrassed."

Millions of women in our nation suffer from hypoesthetic syn-
drome, or a lack of desire to participate in sex due to a problem.
Dr. Marie Robinson, in her book *The Power of Sexual Surrender*,
states that the vast majority of these women and marriages are
suffering only because of a lack of education and a lack of sexual understanding.[5] How sad! How sad to miss the beauty of the
sexual experience in the marriage simply because a husband and
wife aren't learning about each other and themselves, together.

Solutions

The job of the husband is to seek an understanding of the difficulties that are getting in the way of his wife's sexual experience.

Although that might seem like an impossible assignment when his wife appears to have no sexual needs, that husband must take this task very seriously. He might find that his approach to their sexual relationship has made her feel used and demeaned. And even though she might not be able to express that to his satisfaction, he will just have to believe her and be willing to adopt a more sensitive approach.

The wife in this situation must display a willingness to risk. She must risk discussing their sex life, even though it may make her feel like they are discussing an area of personal failure. It is more likely to be an area of unanswered questions than failure. It is *their* area of difficulty, not just hers.

As a couple becomes more willing to communicate, to risk being vulnerable, and to love unconditionally, they will experience greater and greater relational and sexual fulfillment. It is our hope that, not only will they rejoice when they reach the destination, but that they will also cherish the time spent together wrestling through the difficult questions and answers.

Summary

1. There are many reasons that could lead a wife to become uninterested in the sexual relationship.
2. The reasons could originate in a childhood experience or they could come from marital experiences.
3. Couples need to risk looking into and discussing these reasons before they can find solutions.
4. This is a journey that must be taken together, without pointing fingers. It's a marital problem, not the problem of one of the spouses. They're experiencing the results of the problem together. They need to work on the problem together.

Making Sense of the Sexual Puzzle

1. If your wife seems uninterested in your sexual relationship, what can you do to help her discuss the causes?
2. What do you do to make it difficult for your wife to talk about this topic?
3. What can you do to help her feel more comfortable talking about this?
4. What are some possible approaches that you might use?

CHAPTER 14

When He's Not Interested

I don't know what happened to our sex life," Deana said through her tears. "Ralph just isn't interested anymore. During our first couple years of marriage we had what I would think was a normal sex life. Then he just seemed to lose interest altogether. We went from making love a couple times a week to a couple times a month, and now ... now it's probably not a couple times a year."

Deana had finally just stopped trying to arouse Ralph's interest. She had paraded in front of him in a very provocative nightgown, but Ralph pretended not to notice and kept watching television. Something had happened to Ralph that seemed to completely cut off his interest in sex. Deana had no idea what was going on inside her husband because he didn't want to talk about it. Every time she brought it up, Ralph told her she was crazy or that her timing was always wrong. No matter what timing she tried to adjust to, it was never quite right. He wouldn't talk about the fact that they hadn't made love in months or even admit that anything was wrong.

A Difficult Topic for Discussion

Most men find it very difficult to discuss the fact that for some reason they are no longer interested in the sexual intimacy of their marriage. They often view the very discussion as an attack on their manhood.

We live in a very sexual culture, a culture that often feeds things into the male mind via the sexual window of his consciousness. Commercials aimed at the male often use a sexually suggestive woman to grab his attention. Quiz shows regularly employ young women dressed in tight-fitting gowns to help carry things across the stage. And what do cheerleaders really have to do with the Dallas Cowboys' victories?

If sexual prowess, and thus interest in sex, is such a significant part of the male machismo in our culture, the idea of not being interested in sex is very unmasculine. "I feel like there must be something wrong with me as a man," Ralph finally admitted to the counselor after their hour alone was almost up. It was only after he began to realize that his years of silence had left Deana with the wrong impression that he finally admitted that his interest just wasn't there anymore. Since Ralph used to be interested in making love with Deana and now he wasn't, she was left with only one thought: He was having an affair.

"Oh, that's ridiculous," Ralph lashed back, feeling boxed into a corner. "Something *has* happened to our sex life, but it certainly doesn't have anything to do with another woman.

"The whole thing seems crazy to me. Most husbands would give anything to have a wife who walks through the living room dressed in a sexy nightgown. I know that there are other guys who have to beg their wives to make love. Here I am hoping she doesn't do something that I'm expected to respond to. I find myself dreading some bedtimes."

Ralph went on to say that he didn't know why the desire had left him. "Sometimes at work I think about it, but when it's ten o'clock at night I'm just not interested. When I told that to Deana, she immediately assumed that I was interested in somebody at work. Believe me, nothing could be further from the truth. But when she gets all defensive about it after I try to talk to her about it, I feel like it's just not worth hurting her anymore. This thing has become a real big issue, and I'd rather avoid dealing with it altogether."

This couple had two problems. The first was that Ralph felt his lack of interest in sex indicated a lack of masculinity. Hence, he didn't want to talk about it. Once he was willing to risk talking about it with the help of a third party, he began to explore the reasons for his dampened interest.

Causes of Sexual Apathy

Many men go through seasons of their marriage where they seem to lose interest in sex. For Ralph and Deana a helpful way to stimulate communication on this topic was to take the immediate focus off of them and put it on a list of possible reasons. There are many issues that can hamper a man's sexual interest. A man dealing with this is often relieved to know that he's not the only one with this difficulty and that there are often external causes.

Men dealing with this problem often feel very isolated. Women who are dealing with sexual issues in their marriage will often find another woman to talk to about it. Men don't easily discuss this difficulty with friends. Picture this. A man says to his friends, "Hey! Before we start bowling tonight I want to ask you guys something. Have any of you recently lost interest in sex?" That's a hard scene to picture! Men are often left all alone as they look for the reasons. Seeing that there is a possible list of reasons can be very helpful.

Job Pressures

Many times job pressures cause more difficulties and depression than a man and his wife realize. Some men get to the point where they define who they are by their occupation or profession more than by any other part of their life. When their job is in jeopardy, or they have even lost their job, it can cause some men to shut down sexually.

"I didn't feel like I was a man anymore," remembers Paul. "When Eastern Airlines went under and I was no longer flying, it took me a long time to regroup. Sitting around the house waiting for PanAm Airlines to call me for work was very depressing. When I wasn't working, it was like something inside said I didn't deserve certain things because I wasn't providing like a man ought to provide. Margaret thought she was helping by trying to cheer me up, but she wasn't. In fact, when she would try to set up romantic evenings it just made me feel worse. For some reason, after all these years, I was no longer interested in making love. I'm not sure whether I wasn't interested or just didn't think I deserved it. Whatever the cause, our sex life got put on the shelf for those ten months."

Pressures from losing a job or the stress of not being able to pay bills can bend a man over to the point where he becomes depressed and uninterested in sex. The more a wife seems to try to help her husband by pursuing him sexually, the more he feels pressured and the more he withdraws. This can be a very intense time for a husband and wife because their relationship begins to spiral downward. He feels depressed about his circumstances and his inability to work through them. This causes him to back away from sex with his wife. At this point, she tries to help her husband by making him feel worthy and appealing. She pursues him sexually and he turns her away because he's depressed. This causes her to feel rejected and him to feel more depressed. "I felt like even more of a loser," Paul remembered. "She would only be trying to help me feel better and I'd turn away and say something like, 'Not tonight, Honey. I just don't feel like it.' Then she'd become depressed. I was rolling down this hill of depression and I was pulling my wife with me."

The stress and pressure of life can leave a man feeling like life is beating him up and there's nothing he can do about it. Other men might feel helpless as professional opportunities pass them by. When these circumstances persist for long periods of time, the events can affect more than a man's approach to his job. His feelings of a lack of occupational worth can follow him home and have an effect on his marriage. Under these circumstances, it is often better for a wife to be open to her husband's lead rather than to take the leadership and try to pull him out. He might already feel "led to death." Some men feel as if they should be the pullers rather than the pulled.

No More Chase

Other men find the chase of the relationship to be the most enticing part. When he and his wife were dating or engaged, he thrived on chasing after her and doing everything he could do to win her over. But then, shortly after the wedding, when he was no longer chasing, he became bored. To him sex was just the trophy of the victory.

This is an immature orientation that can be very difficult to deal with. This husband finds his "ejaculation" in the pursuit of the relationship rather than the relationship itself. Once he's obtained the prize, this husband often pulls away from the relationship and the sexual part of the marriage altogether. He finds other games to play. Softball or other sports become his challenge. This is not to say that all men who want to play softball or other sports after they are married are behaving immaturely. But there are some men who are so enticed by pursuing the "win," that shortly after the wedding, they find sports more exciting than the marriage and sex. At least the game provides them with a challenge.

These are husbands who have no idea what a relationship is all about. Perhaps in the home that they grew up in, the children were loved only for how well they performed or how hard they worked. Some young men received approval from their parents or parent only when they won. When they won at grades or they won at sports, their parents made them feel worthy. Thus they worked hard to win the prize of their bride. But once they won her, they had no idea how to have an ongoing relationship. They won the trophy, but they didn't know that they were supposed to do something with it (or her). Consequently they left the trophy at home and went out looking to get more approval by winning more contests. The game of the relationship is just too confusing and unwinnable. It's easier to win at other things.

Men who do not understand relationships often need to go for personal help before they can work on the marriage. They need to first overcome their lack of understanding about the purpose and the need for relationships in general. This difficulty of developing in-depth relationships might not be limited to their marriage. It might also permeate their relationship with their children. Many of the men's organizations today are trying to help men see that need.

Obsessive Sex

"Compulsive sex activity can be just as destructive as addiction to drugs or alcohol," concludes one researcher.[1] Sexual addiction can eventually destroy the sexual relationship between a husband and a wife and eventually the marriage itself. Sex addicts experience a euphoria from the sexual experience that is similar to the high addicts receive from drugs. Initially a wife can be made to feel as if there is something wrong with her when she is not able to respond to the sexual advances from her husband two and three times a day. Without talking about this conflict and realizing that there is a problem that needs professional attention, a husband could find himself looking elsewhere to relieve this sexual tension. This is a difficulty that needs immediate professional help. If a wife cannot get her husband to go for help, she should go alone to find out what she can do to deal with the problem.

The relationship in this case becomes so strained that a man might shut down at home, only because he is constantly sexually active at work and in his neighborhood. This malady is much more common than people realize. Again, it is a difficulty that requires immediate professional help.

Strong Leader

Some men are strong leaders and are very controlled in everything they do. It is next to impossible for them to show any weakness or admit to needing any help. Their leadership skills may be in the area of domination and intimidation. This man could be a captain of industry or a foreman on a construction job. Whatever the environment, this man stays very controlled in his responses to life's circumstances. He is used to having people come to him to get help at overcoming their problems.

One of the most significant areas of a man's life over which he has very little control can be his marriage. He may be able to call all the shots at work, but his marriage calls for compromise. His work might be a place where he projects an image of needing nothing, but that won't work at home. In fact, his wife might find that the sexual part of their marriage is the only area in which she has any say. This man is not used to asking or compromising. When he has to compromise, he might feel like he is really showing weakness. Instead of asking her if she wants to make love, he waits for her to come to him, as if she is the only one with a need. It's outside his controlling character to admit he needs her for anything. When they hit a point in their relationship where she is tired of fanning his already flaming ego by pursuing him sexually, he has to make a decision. Either he pursues her and admits his need for her, or he goes without making love.

This can be a very humbling, though valuable, experience for this particular husband and a growing experience for the marriage. If the husband finally decides to swallow his pride and admit that he needs his wife, he'll do a great service to his ego. If this husband decides that he doesn't know everything he needs to know about marriage and asks for her input, it will be a much needed time of maturing. In this case, the marriage can be a great finishing school for this husband. He will be forced to let go of some of his control.

Another husband, however, will fight this posture of blending. It will be very difficult for him to admit that he needs anybody. It will be equally hard for him to let go of the control of his pride and admit he doesn't have all the answers. This husband might decide to go without, rather than go further in the relationship.

Domineering Wife

Marriages with domineering wives have been the source of comedy on television for many years. In real life these are not humorous situations. Some men are married to wives who verbally castrate them and make them feel inept and powerless. This domineering may be overt and obvious, but it may also be very subtle.

One wife didn't see that the things she did were an affront to her husband's masculinity. She truly thought she was helping. She was helping him get a better job and she was helping him do a better job at his church work. In fact, she was in charge of her ladies' church group and wondered why he had dropped out of the men's committee he had served on. After all, she worked hard to get him on that very prominent group. Over the years he was made to feel that she was better at everything than he was. He just couldn't compete. For his emotional preservation he just backed away. Next to her he felt inadequate.

As discussed earlier, God defined the marriage relationship in Ephesians 5:33. The wife is to respect her husband. Whether he is respectable or not, she is to cultivate this attitude in order to build their relationship. Part of his need is to feel respected.

This particular husband felt unworthy next to his wife and unromantic around her, so he eventually backed away from her entirely. He stayed away from a sexual relationship with her for many years. Unfortunately, there was a woman at the place where he worked who thought he was very capable in the things he did. She actually respected his opinion. After years without a sexual relationship with his domineering wife, this man caved in to an extramarital affair. He felt he could not be sexually involved with a woman who treated him like a child, but he found himself drawn to a woman who treated him like a man. He was a sitting duck for this tragedy.

Rejected by Life

We all choose our reactions to life's circumstances. Certain circumstances motivate some men to work harder, while those very same circumstances seem to crush other men. This is not because the former men are stronger and the latter are weaker, but simply because they are different and function with different personalities.

Some husbands find it difficult to come home to their wives for comfort when they have been dealt rejection by the outside world. Not the rejection of losing a job, but the rejection that goes along with their job. There are certain professions that lend themselves to the ongoing battle between rejection and acceptance. The most obvious profession would be sales. The man who sells life insurance understands that he must get past the rejection in order to get to the person who actually wants his product. He will never find that person without asking many if they are interested. In the process he will be rejected.

Other professions are less obvious sources of rejection. Take pastors, for instance. Their profession is not supposed to be a numbers game. But often whether or not a church is growing numerically greatly affects a pastor's sense of self-worth. Every pastor must deal with the possible and even probable rejection of his message by those to whom he preaches.

This rejection can affect the marriages of these men. Many have been known to shut down sexually without even realizing it. Instead of escaping into their marriage, they escape from the relationship. Relationships have become dangerous to them because of the rejection they feel in their relationships with their co-workers or congregations, so they shut down relationally and sexually. Many of these men renew their sexual relationships with their wives as their career or church picks up. When they no longer perceive themselves as being rejected by their client or parish, they are more comfortable in their marriage.

Often this difficulty needs only to be identified. The man needs help seeing what he's doing, and then he needs help realizing that his wife is not one who will reject. It is also helpful for him to know that he is not alone in this difficult quest to grow a client base or church. Some husbands are helped just by knowing that others in their field are going through the same difficulties. Often men only hear about those whose careers and churches take off. The ninety percent who are struggling don't make front page of the trade journals.

Appearance

Weight is a very dominant power in our culture. Magazines and movies feature models that none of us could ever look like. Some men shut down sexually because of their weight. Other men shut down because their wives are overweight. Often when this issue is analyzed, it's not a matter of an overweight spouse being unappealing as much as it is a form of punishment.

One man believed that he had been so undisciplined in letting his body become overweight that he didn't deserve to make love to his wife. Another husband felt that if his wife really loved him and respected him, she'd do something about the weight she had gained; he believed that he wasn't interested in making love with his wife because of her weight. He even let her know who of their friends he felt were the women who had respect for their husbands and themselves. His feeling was that if a woman respected and loved her spouse, she wouldn't let her body go. He judged women solely by their figures.

Both forms of punishment are very damaging. A husband who feels overweight and unworthy must either work on his appearance or work on a realistic attitude. But he cannot deny his marriage a sexual relationship simply because he doesn't feel good about himself.

A husband who feels that he has the right to punish his wife because she doesn't meet his physical specifications is arrogant and immature. Heaven help his home if she is in a car accident and is disfigured. We have no right to respond to a spouse in a way that would punish them for being overweight. The same passage in Ephesians that commands wives to respect their husbands also commands husbands to love their wives. They are to love them unconditionally, not because they lose the proper amount of weight or look a certain way.

A similar problem that seems to shut some husbands down sexually comes from another area of the home life. "She keeps the house like such a pigpen that I can hardly even look at her when we get home at night. I don't know what she thinks a house is supposed to look like, but this isn't it. It's hard to have any kind of relationship when our home looks like this."

This husband was also punishing his wife, although he didn't realize it. She wasn't doing what he perceived she was supposed to do, so he just left the house and went to the gym to work out. He didn't help her with the house. Instead he left her to do it herself, and he shut down their relationship altogether. He punished her by not responding to their sexual needs. He punished himself by not allowing for his needs. He continually punished the whole relationship by avoiding instead of helping. Their marriage became a disaster as he became more and more angry and she became more and more distant. Now almost a year after the divorce he has been forced to reflect: "How could I have been so self-centered?" Appearance of the person or house can be a catalyst to shut down sexual desire in some men.

Too Hard to Figure Out

More than shut down, some men just quit. They can't figure out their wives' needs, and they become very frustrated. Many of their evenings, when he thought that they would be making love, have ended in disaster. He doesn't know what he did to upset her, or what he didn't do to draw her toward him. He had no idea, and he got tired of failing.

What this type of husband didn't do was risk learning. He didn't ask for help. He didn't sit down and read a book about the marriage relationship. He just assumed that if he couldn't figure it out on his own, he and his wife must just be incompatible. He quit. For years they stayed married and he said to himself, "Well, that's just the way she is. This whole marriage thing is highly over-rated anyway."

Instead of saying, "Let me help you understand how different we are," some wives just sit waiting for their husbands to figure it out. More than one wife has said, "If I have to tell him what to do, I don't want it!" They both failed.

Instead of working on learning more about his marriage, a husband may shut it down and watch sexually explicit movies and videos instead. By watching his culture and listening to his friends talk, he concludes, "Isn't this what every man does to deal with his sexual needs?" No it's not. It's not what God planned when he put us together in marriage. This man hides from the prospect of a great marriage and a great sexual relationship. He doesn't understand his wife's needs and he's not willing to ask for help.

Guilt

There are certainly other emotional inhibitors that a man might have to deal with. One final one, however, is probably the saddest of all. The man who shuts down sexually because of guilt over something in his past.

It could be his distant past. He may be living with the memory of having been sexually abused when he was younger. He may wonder if the molestation he endured was a result of his own homosexual signals he gave to an uncle or a neighbor. Childhood molestation often leaves significant questions in a man's mind about his own sexual orientation. The emotional scars have been there for so long that they have become distorted.

"I was afraid to talk to someone about this whole issue," a counselee confessed. "I was afraid I would find out that I was gay. Even though I love my wife and have no inclination toward men, I was so traumatized by my uncle that I wondered if maybe I had encouraged the whole thing. I just wanted to keep it all inside. But when I couldn't respond to Betty, I knew I had to do something about it. Coming for counseling has been one of the most difficult things I've ever done, and one of the most rewarding."

Past trauma often comes back to haunt present relationships. For many men there's an even greater fear of revealing this past to their spouses. How will she feel if she finds out? A past trauma also has a way of becoming distorted. A little child can feel that he did something to encourage the molestation by a trusted and respected relative. As the years go by, dredging up the experience becomes more difficult. Difficult but mandatory.

Guilt from more recent events can also have the same effect. A husband who has had an affair or a one-night stand, perhaps while away on business, can be so overpowered by guilt that he becomes debilitated. He feels so wretched that he can no longer respond to his wife. In fact, he finds it difficult to even look at her.

It's not only the guilt of the affair, but perhaps the guilt of potentially bringing home a sexually transmitted disease. What if his weakness and sin cause his wife to become diseased? This tremendous guilt has led some husbands to shut down sexually rather than open up and confess. Yes, the trauma of confessing the violation would be incredible. But the long-term effects of shutting down the relationship can be even worse.

"I thought I'd get past it," Arnold confessed to his wife. "I thought if I didn't say anything, eventually I would be able to look you in the eye and we could get on with our marriage. I guess what I'm saying is that I thought I could get away with this horrible thing I'd done, without hurting you. But I couldn't. Things just got worse. The guilt was killing me and affecting every area of my life. When I began pulling away, I began hurting you just as much as I was hurting."

Exposure to Pollutants

One of the biggest causes of sexual dissatisfaction in our culture today is the sexual pollutants that enter into the male mind. Pornography has become an accepted form of male entertainment in many circles. This pollutant leaves a man with a mental picture of the sexual relationship which not only demeans women, but is grossly out of step with the blending process that making love is supposed to be. Pornography depicts women doing things for or to men, any men. The fact that it is filmed and then watched is a tremendous violation of intimacy. But then, that's the purpose of pornography, to violate the intimacy of sexuality.

Making love in the marriage is a blend of a husband and wife doing things for each other. Pornography depicts an immature taking, while sex in marriage is supposed to grow in its sacrificial loving and giving. Pornography will only leave a man very unsatisfied in his sexual relationship at home. It is a compulsion that can turn into an addiction. Eventually a husband will be forced to choose between his pornographic appetite or marital sex. Sadly, many men have chosen to walk away from their marriage.

Physical Inhibitors

Past sexual experience, a job, self-esteem, or a man's attitude toward the events and people around him—all these things can close in on him and cause him to back away from the intimacy of a sexual relationship with his wife. These are emotional inhibitors, but there are also physical inhibitors that can have a grave impact on the sexual relationship.

Impotence

Perhaps the best known sexual difficulty for the male is impotence. This includes both difficulty in achieving and difficulty in maintaining an erection. Nothing is more frustrating or damaging to the masculinity of some men than the problem of impotence. Unfortunately, many men subscribe to our culture's definition of masculinity—sexual prowess. Impotence, therefore, would seem to be the opposite of masculinity. That logic makes about as much sense as baldness affecting a man's intelligence!

The biggest obstacle to overcoming impotence is a man's tendency to avoid sex so he won't have to deal with his problem. Many men feel so emasculated by the thought of being impotent that they won't even discuss it. Instead they choose to avoid sex and refuse to face the difficulty and pursue a solution.

The first step in solving the problem is for a couple to own the problem as "theirs" and not simply "his." Many cases of impotence are correctable. The inability to gain or keep an erection is generally a physiological problem that can often be remedied by a physician. If no physical cause can be found, a couple would be wise to seek counseling.

Ejaculatory Problems

The point of this book is not to offer medical advice, but rather to encourage couples to work at achieving the greatest sexual relationship they can possibly have. In some cases this may be hampered by problems of premature ejaculation or the inability to reach ejaculation. These may be caused by various medical procedures, such as for prostate cancer. The key here is to pursue answers.

Due to the sensitivity of the men with this malady, many men just shut down and avoid the issue. They avoid sex altogether rather than talk about their problem with a physician. This is self-defeating behavior. Seek solutions, not seclusion.

Solutions

1. Open the Lines of Communication

Often a wife thinks that she can help her husband by trying various ways to arouse him sexually. When that doesn't work she feels rejected and he feels more distant. They don't talk and further compound the problem.

Lack of communication leads a spouse to only one conclusion: I must be the source of the problem. Open the lines of communication, if for no other reason than to relieve a wife of the burden of believing that she has done something to cause her husband's lack of interest in sex. "When Jack wouldn't talk to me about why he didn't seem interested in making love anymore," one wife said, "it led me to think that I just didn't turn him on anymore." Another wife thought that her husband must be having an affair. If it was any other problem, she was sure he would be able to talk to her about it. Unfortunately, she was wrong. He didn't feel able to talk about it.

Very little can happen until the lines of communication are opened. Then a husband and wife can share the problem rather than withdrawing from each other. Communication within the marriage is the first step.

2. Identify the Difficulty

Can the difficulty be identified, and if so, can it be resolved? This conversation needs to progress slowly because most men cannot get to deeper levels of communication as quickly as many women can. Talking about sex is about as deep a level of communication as a man can imagine, especially communication about something as personal and, from his perspective, unmasculine as his lack of interest.

During this period of communication it is important for a husband to realize that he is loved and respected whether or not this issue is resolved. The only thing that might hamper that respect could be an unwillingness to try to seek answers. This time of communication is not just to resolve the problems of the sex life in the marriage. More importantly, the communication is to restore and build the whole relationship in the marriage.

3. Make an Appointment

The difficulty might be more physical than it is emotional. If so, a urologist should be able to identify the problem. One man who had recently gone through treatment for prostate cancer indicated that he was depressed about his sexual difficulties since his cancer treatment. But as depressed as he was, his doctor was able to offer him help for the time being and offer the encouragement that his condition would be back to normal in a matter of months. "I was just glad to know there was a light at the end of the tunnel. If I hadn't talked to him about it, I would have assumed that our sex life was over."

4. Get Good Counsel

Be willing to seek help. It is very important that this help is sought only from sources that share the same philosophy of life as the couple. Books and counselors should certainly be used, but they should be Christian books and counselors. These counselors or resource materials have a basic premise that sex in marriage is a gift from God and that God has a special plan for it.

5. Maintain Intimacy

Many marriages might have been built on their sex life. Then something comes crashing in and devastates that part of the couple's relationship. Whether or not a solution for the difficulty is found, the key issue is the intimacy of the love. The physical love is very significant, but the relational intimacy is the glue that will bind a marriage together for years to come. Commit to learn ways of loving each other, whether or not the sexual part of the marriage is repaired. There are times when every couple must realize that the deeper the intimacy in a marriage goes the more the sexual aspect becomes the icing on the cake, not the cake itself. Take steps to deal with the problem, but commit to love each other regardless of the outcome.

Summary

1. There are many possible explanations that can help a couple understand why a husband might shut down sexually. Some are emotional and some are physical.
2. The most important step in dealing with a husband's lack of interest in sex is to open the lines of communication. This area of communication can be very sensitive for a husband, so the process will need to be handled very gently and slowly.
3. It is often helpful to look at a list of possible reasons for this lack of interest, since many husbands would not be able to label the reason if asked.
4. Don't be afraid to seek outside help when working on this difficulty.

Making Sense of the Sexual Puzzle

1. Look at the list of possible reasons for a husband to shut down sexually in his marriage. Of all the possibilities on this list, which area could be the one to affect your marriage?

2. What are the areas of your life that could hamper or have hampered your sexual relationship?
3. What area of sexual difficulty is the hardest for you to talk about?
4. In the past, what was the best place, time, and situation where you were able to have an intimate discussion about your sexual relationship?

PART THREE

Having Sex or Making Love

CHAPTER 15

Learning to Love

W e're not making love!" Janie cried to her husband, Philip. "How could anybody say this is love? Every few nights we're just meeting each other's needs. Sometimes yours and then sometimes mine. No! Most of the time yours, and on rare occasions, mine. Most of the time we don't even talk to each other before we get into bed. This isn't making love! There's got to be something more than this obligatory sexual relationship we've developed."

Janie was upset with the direction their sexual relationship had gone. She didn't realize that most marriages travel this road. At some point, a couple has to move from just having sex to actually making love.

Having Sex

The sexual experience is motivated by tremendous biological drives. A husband receives incredible anticipatory excitement and then biological pleasure from an ejaculation. His wife, in turn, can experience the intimacy of being physically close, as well as her own biological excitement culminating in an orgasm.

In the early stages of a marriage, this sexual experience should be a wonderful part of the relationship. The young husband looks forward to the biological release of sex, while his wife anticipates both the relationship leading up to the sexual interplay and then her own orgasm experience. During the early months of a marriage, this sexual excitement can overshadow the difficulties a couple will experience while adjusting to each other.

The time will come, however, when each couple will turn a corner. A husband will realize that he really doesn't need a lot of relational foreplay before the sex. In fact, he will find that he could go all day without even talking to his new wife, yet he still wants to interact with her sexually that night, even that afternoon if she's available. Without realizing it, he will gradually bypass the relationship to get to the sex.

His wife, on the other hand, becomes disenchanted. She feels used by her husband who seems to ignore her until they are near the bedroom. In the past she was trading her desire for relationship and sex for his desire for sex. It worked for a season, but now, without the relationship coming from him, she feels short-changed.[1]

This is the time in a marriage where a couple will decide whether they are going to stay in this sexual conflict by ignoring the inequity of the relationship, or they are going to move up to the next stage—making love.

Making Love

Once Janie had told her husband that she was sure that they weren't making love, he was initially very frustrated with the whole conversation. In his frustration, this young husband fired back a statement, right in front of the counselor, that typifies their difficulty: "Just what do you think 'making love' means anyway? I give up! Who knows what love means?!"

The Originator of love went to the trouble of defining this word for all who would care to understand it. God defined love in the Bible, in 1 Corinthians 13:4–8:

> Love is patient, love is kind.
> It does not envy, it does not boast, it is not proud.
> It is not rude, it is not self-seeking,
> it is not easily angered,
> it keeps no record of wrongs.
> Love does not delight in evil but rejoices with the truth.
> It always protects, always trusts,
> always hopes, always perseveres.
> Love never fails.

This passage refers to the word or action of love in general: It defines what "love" is. But it also describes the difference between having sex and making love. If this definition of love is applied to a couple's sexual response to each other, each one may see the need to focus on the other person when making love.

Before a couple can start learning to take the step from *having sex* to *making love,* they must understand what true love is. According to the definition given us by the Author of love, love is something you *do,* rather than something you *feel.* Love isn't something that I feel because my spouse is wonderful to me, great at sex, or looks fantastic. In addition, I love someone even when that person has not taken an equally loving action toward me. The definition says that "love is kind" and that "love doesn't keep a record of wrongs." Love is an unconditional action.

Love as Sexual Expression

I will never forget watching Janie's husband as he tried to process this whole conversation about "love versus sex." Finally he asked, "But how does this apply to our sexual relationship? This is all nice and philosophical, but when you get right down to it, how do I make it work in the sexual context?"

If a man's biology is urgent in the demands to get on with the physical side of having sex with his wife, he needs to slow down and remember her needs. If she wants to spend time in the evening talking rather than watching television, as a form of foreplay, he needs to slow down. Remember, *love is patient.* Whether or not he understands this need is not important. Love doesn't have to understand the reason. It only needs to hear the need and respond accordingly. Love is like that because *love is kind.*

In the same manner, Janie might not understand why her husband would like to spend that time talking or relating with her while she is dressed in a provocative nightgown. "Not all the time," her husband explained, "but every now and then. That would be exciting for me." Janie didn't understand his reasoning. It did nothing for her to parade downstairs in a provocative nightgown. She really didn't like sitting there dressed like that because she felt funny when he stared at her body. She didn't look the way she wanted to look anymore. There was the difficulty of her pride to overcome. "Why should he need this? It makes me feel like an object." However, real love does not get hindered or constrained by pride. *It is not proud,* according to the definition.

What should they do when Janie and her husband disagree on something that one of them wants to do sexually? First of all, *love is not easily angered.* How they discuss the issue can demonstrate their love. The way they treat each other needs to show that their attitude toward each other is far more important than getting their way on a particular sexual issue. This is because, by definition, *love is not rude,* nor is it *self-seeking.*

Often the past is a difficult area to overcome when it comes to working on a couple's sex life. But the past needs to be left in the past. Not just in discussion, but also in one's thoughts. "I have a hard time giving myself totally to our sex life," one woman admitted. "Every time we make love, I hold myself back thinking that if I get overly excited, he'll try to push me into doing things I don't want to do, like he used to do."

Her husband broke in. "How long has it been since I tried to get you to do some of those things?" As it turned out, they both agreed that it had been more than a couple of years. She had allowed her memories to inhibit her sexually. But true love *keeps no record of wrongs.*

Sexual love *doesn't delight in evil.* One of the areas that delighting in evil could refer to would be pornographic materials, or any materials that take the sexual realm of the marriage outside one's own bedroom. Many times, that will include movies that are not rated X, but which still look in on another couple's intimacy. Watching another couple have sex is taking that scene outside our own bedroom into their bedroom. To get excited about, or to delight in watching, another couple having sex is not love.

"I never understood looking at sexually explicit movies to be blatantly wrong," confessed a man beginning the long journey from sex to making love, "until I realized that I would be embarrassed to be watching these movies if Christ returned. That's when I understood that I was not delighting myself only in my wife."

This man had gotten used to getting excited or delighting himself in outside materials and then having sex with his wife to fulfill that excitement. He had chosen not to delight himself in his wife. Thus he wasn't making love, he was having sex. He was being *rude* to his wife and *self-seeking* as he *delighted* himself in *evil.*

The Bible is always the ultimate word on the definition of evil. When, after a search of what the Bible has to say, a couple can't find a definitive answer to a specific problem, the next step is to figuratively put Christ in a chair next to you. He created our sexuality for us to enjoy, but is the thing being considered a use of our sexuality that he would be pleased with? Will this action preserve the purity of our sexual expression toward each other and bring both of us happiness?

Ultimately It Takes Two

Making the transition from having sex in a marriage to making love is best done when both spouses are interested in taking the step together. But notice that the biblical definition of love includes the word *patience*. One spouse might learn how to love much faster than the other spouse.

When one spouse decides to approach their sexual relationship with the other person's happiness as a priority, frustration can result. One spouse might feel like he or she is trying, while the other spouse is not. In fact, initially the spouse who doesn't seem to be trying quite as hard can be perceived as taking advantage of the other spouse.

"I know Janie thinks that I'm the one receiving all the pleasure," said Philip. "But I'm not. I'm trying to think of her. But it doesn't come as easily to me as it does to her. She has such a servant attitude. I'm really trying to learn how to put her first, not just sexually, but in everything we do. It's just taking me longer."

One spouse is naturally going to be more adept at readjusting his or her sexual attitude than the other spouse. But remember, love is never conditional. A loving spouse will not say, "See how much I do for you? I work all day, and then I come home tired and try to understand your needs. What are *you* doing?" *Love never boasts.* Nor does love say, "Here I am making all these adjustments to learn to make you happy, and you don't seem to be doing anything," because, by definition, *love does not envy* the other person. To love another person is to take an action regardless of his or her reaction.

Janie brought up a difficult question: "What if Philip never tries? What if I'm the only one working at learning to make love?"

Never is a loaded word. For the time being, making love means that Janie's sexual response to her husband is not dependent upon her needs being met first. In fact, the definition instructs us to love someone and protect the relationship with the hope that one day the other spouse will feel loved enough to risk trying to make love, rather than just having sex. Love *always protects, always trusts, always hopes, and always perseveres.*

One night when Janie seemed to indicate that she wanted to make love, but fell asleep instead, her husband had to decide to love her. Disappointed as he was, he had to decide to recommit his desire to love his wife. That's because *love never fails.* Love is not a one-time decision. Rather loving requires constant, daily recommitment.

Loving is not easy. Perhaps that's why God created such a wonderful prize at the end of the process. Not the prize of an orgasm or ejaculation. As wonderful as those may be, the prize is far greater. That is the prize of loving and eventually being loved.

Perspective

In order to do this seemingly impossible task of putting the other person's sexual needs before one's own sexual desires, a new perspective must be learned. We are taught to learn and understand our own needs and wants. Then we are taught, in our culture, to be assertive to get our desires and needs met. In the Bible, Paul countered this philosophy in Galatians 5:13 with advice to "serve one another in love."

This change in perspective is really an active decision to truly love another person. To change that perspective a spouse must learn what his or her spouse's particular needs and desires are and which of those desires he or she can meet.

"It was difficult for me to imagine why Janie would want to spend a couple hours sitting in front of the fireplace talking, when we could be upstairs in bed together," Philip admitted. "I just had to learn to listen to what she was saying she would like to do, and then to do what I could to make those desires my priority."

The Power

The selfless attitude that is necessary to truly love another person can only be acquired with the power found in a life committed to Jesus Christ.

For a couple to learn to take the step from having sex to making love, they must adopt a new perspective. That selfless perspective will be impossible to maintain under one's own power. The power to maintain that perspective comes from the Author and Creator of that love (Zechariah 4:6). A couple's opportunity to experience making love will be directly proportional to their experience with Christ. Therein is the power to put self aside for the happiness of another person.

Summary

1. Having sex is the first stage of a marriage relationship. This early sexual experience is initially all that a couple needs or understands.
2. At some point in the early years of the marriage one or both partners come to the realization that there must be more than just the physical expression and ecstasy of sex. At this stage a crisis often brings a discussion about the sexual relationship in the marriage.
3. This crisis or discussion can be a great catalyst to making the transition from having sex to making love.
4. Making love requires a mature understanding of love based on 1 Corinthians 13.

Making Sense of the Sexual Puzzle

1. What is your spouse's most pressing sexual need? Are you willing to meet that need?
2. What personal perspective do you need to change to make the transition from having sex to making love?
3. When is a good time for you and your spouse to get away from the house to discuss this necessary step?
4. Why do you hesitate to have this discussion? What can you do about these hesitations?

CHAPTER 16
Make It an Event

T hings were different when we dated in college," Rosemary said one night.

Dutiful husband that I am, I took my cue. "What do you mean?"

Rosemary replied, "You took more time to prepare to be with me back then. It was as if you made love to me back then, but without having sex. Now we do have sex, but you don't make love to me."

"What in the world does that mean?"

"In college," Rosemary explained, "when you knew we were going to be doing something together that evening, you would wash the car, take a shower, and even shave a second time in a day, all for me. Now it's different. If we're going to go someplace for dinner, you race in the door from work, put your briefcase down, check the mail, tell me you're ready to go, and we're out the door. Same shirt and tie you wore all day, and same dirty car. If you were coming home, knowing we were going to spend an evening out with another couple, you'd get here in time to take a shower. If we were going to pick them up in your car, you would have seen to it that it was clean. If it's just me, both you and the car remain dirty!"

Her words made me stop and think. I was not making our time together an event. I was treating it very flippantly. I would probably be treating our time together much more seriously when 11:00 that night rolled around, however.

I learned a valuable lesson that day. Lovemaking needs to be prepared for like a special event. We need to set aside time where we focus only on the other person and his or her desires.

After reading Joseph Dillow's book *Solomon on Sex*, we decided to call this kind of a night of focus a "Solomon Night." Solomon nights don't need to happen every time you make love. Let me rephrase that. They can't possibly happen every time you make love. Life doesn't afford every couple an opportunity to clear the deck for a whole evening dedicated to making love. But this kind of dedication to the event, or a Solomon Night, needs to happen regularly. If it does not, your lovemaking experience will become stale and ordinary.

Sexual Instruction from the Song of Songs

The book called Song of Songs has been interpreted in various ways, as we discussed in an earlier chapter. But one of its very significant functions is to act as an instructional or procedural manual for married couples. It illustrates some very basic procedures for making love. In fact, these instructions might just be the defining gestures that differentiate sex from making love.

The "love" passage in 1 Corinthians offered the reader some principles of how to love another person in everyday life. The Song of Songs illustrates those principles through the dialogue of two lovers.

The Atmosphere

The Song of Songs begins with talk of love between the bridegroom and his bride. In addition to the beautiful way they verbally love each other here, we get a quick glimpse at the bed chamber.

At that time in Israel, as well as the rest of the East, it would have been the custom of a well-to-do husband to build a special bridal chamber. As he built this special room, Solomon imported cedar trees from his new wife's home region. He went to great lengths to make her feel comfortable and cherished.

What does this teach us? In most of our homes today, the master bedroom is anything but a special place for a husband and wife to retreat to. There would be no way for them to lock the door and spend time together. They wouldn't be able to see each other over the laundry piled on the bed! The master bedroom has become a place where things get stored and desks get piled high with the unpaid bills. Hardly the special kind of place that Solomon built for his bride. Hardly a special place for an "event." There would be too many distractions for us to spend time together talking.

The master bedroom is often the last place that we even decorate. After all, why bother, no one even sees it! But we do. This is supposed to be a place where we come for solace and comfort. A place to get away from it all and renew the marriage relationship. A place for privacy without clutter.

When I was a boy, my mother became very ill and died of cancer. Several years later, my dad remarried, and during the engagement he had a new house built. One Saturday, as the house was nearing completion, my dad and I walked through the upstairs of our new home.

"What in the world is this room?" I remember asking my dad. We had just entered a huge room that had another room elevated a few steps up above it and off to the side. "It's the master bedroom," Dad answered. "That area up there is a sitting area. This is a place where Lisa and I will be able to get away together and talk."

When my mom was alive, our old house didn't have anything like that. It was almost as if my dad was taking advantage of having another chance. A tragedy in his life had shown him what it meant to lose something very valuable—the intimacy he shared with my mom. He wasn't going to miss it this second time around. He built a room where he and his wife could get away and have some privacy, not just a bed, but also a place to sit and talk.

The majority of us can't build a new bedroom, but we can certainly see to it that we develop a new attitude toward the use of the bedroom we have. We can look at our bedroom realistically to see if we've done everything we can to keep it from becoming a place for quick sex, rather than relationship and lovemaking.

More Than Preparing a Bedroom

In the Song of Songs, repeated reference is made to the couple preparing themselves for one another and the event of being together. Often mentioned is the fragrance that the woman has adorned herself with especially to please the man.

"If she'd just take a shower before coming to bed it would help," a husband commented. He was laughing nervously when he said it but he obviously wasn't kidding. "It's not much of a turn-on to have her come to bed after she does her aerobics and sits around for a half hour cooling off. Then she wonders why I'm not excited about getting close to her."

Preparing yourself and your surroundings for lovemaking sends a strong message of love to your spouse. Your actions let your lover know that you are willing to do whatever it takes to enhance your lover's pleasure and enrich your time together.

Making Love Means Making Conversation

Song of Songs has something else to teach us: Foreplay begins not with touching, but with talking. These lovers consistently speak to each other using loving, encouraging words. This verbal foreplay must start as non-sexual in nature. It is a time set aside when a couple can talk about the day and renew their relationship after being apart in their daily activities. It is a time to encourage a spouse in areas of his or her life other than just appearance. For example, if a wife has spent the day surrounded by toddlers, and she doesn't feel that she really accomplished anything of value, this is not the time to offer advice such as, "You know I think if you scheduled your day differently and took the phone off the hook, you'd be able to get the house cleaned." This is a time to offer comfort and encouragement such as, "You know, I never really realized how hard it was to get anything done with these two kids under foot until you left me with them that Saturday. I think you're doing great just to spend time with the kids and get supper on the table." This type of conversation is like a soothing bath. Your willingness to listen to your spouse can be a cleansing rinse, gently removing the soil of criticism or frustration. And your words of love can be a healing oil, softening and strengthening the one who receives them. This is a time to verbally caress rather than to correct.

Visual Foreplay

The bride in the Song of Songs is dressed to turn her husband on. When they are in the bed chamber she must be wearing something very revealing and provocative. The bridegroom comments repeatedly on the beauty of her body. Several times he makes reference to the beauty of her breasts. This wife understands her lover well enough to know that he is turned on by visual stimuli. She's going to make sure that he has that opportunity to see her body.

A wife might want to excite her husband with provocative dress that reveals her body, but she might also be very insecure about the way she looks. A woman's self-esteem about her body directly correlates to the way her husband responds to seeing it. The bridegroom in Song of Songs knew the significance of repeatedly telling his bride how beautiful her body was. Hence, the reader is given the impression that she feels comfortable revealing herself to him.

Interestingly, we are not really given a picture of what she looks like. Reading the description the bridegroom gives, one would think she was a cover girl. Probably not. She was just the total focus of his heart, and he made sure she knew it. Hence, he was the total focus of her advances, and she made sure he knew it. Their time of visual and verbal foreplay was very focused on making the other person happy. Notice that no touching has taken place yet. So far, the intimacy has been emotional rather than physical.

Physical Foreplay

"Let his left hand be under my head and his right hand embrace me" (Song of Songs 2:6). This is a beautiful picture of physical foreplay, but it is also instruction from the bride to the bridegroom.

The Hebrew word translated *embrace* also means *to fondle.* The bride is instructing her husband how to touch her in a way that will sexually excite her. She could also move his hand and then instruct him how to touch her. Notice that the focus here is on his listening to better meet her needs.

Physical foreplay is not grabbing another person's body because it feels good to touch. It's not necessarily touching the way you want to touch as much as it is touching the way your spouse wants to be touched. Foreplay is touching done by one spouse to arouse the other spouse. A spouse must listen to the other person's rate of excitement, so as not to go too fast or too slow. "Do not arouse or awaken love until it so desires" (Song of Songs 2:7).

This picture and others in Song of Songs make it apparent that each spouse must instruct the other. The picture here is that they strive to bring each other to complete fulfillment slowly and gently, rather than simply go after their own needs. They are making love long before they have physical intercourse.

If you haven't stopped to read the five or so pages of Song of Songs yet, this is a great time to share it aloud with your spouse. See how the Creator of sexuality envisioned the sexual relationship in marriage. Our hope is that this love story will encourage and motivate you and your spouse to continue to build your sexual relationship and that your marriage will be strengthened as a result.

Summary

1. Making love doesn't just happen by accident. Couples need to set some procedures.
2. Making love needs to be an event.
3. Prepare your surroundings; see that they are attractive and neat. Prepare yourself; take a shower, splash on some cologne, and brush your teeth.
4. Verbal and visual foreplay are a very strategic part of the lovemaking event. Foreplay is relational, encouraging, and instructional.

Making Sense of the Sexual Puzzle

1. What evening and time will you set aside to study Song of Songs and talk about your relationship?
2. If this is something that your spouse won't do, read it alone and search for your role in the lovemaking process.
3. What do you find in Song of Songs that you would like to add to your lovemaking experience?
4. What do you see that the bride or bridegroom in Song of Songs is doing that you need to start doing?

CHAPTER 17

Start Your Own
Affair at Home

Carol and Barry had just finished watching a movie, and they were sitting at either end of the same couch.

As they both stared straight ahead, Carol spoke wistfully. "That couple seemed so happy." She sighed. "Their affair looked absolutely dreamy."

Barry and Carol had been married for fourteen years. They had become apathetic toward their love life and each other. Oh, they were cordial and considerate, but it was a courtesy you would show a casual acquaintance. Somehow the romantic side of their relationship had been lost.

Carol's comment surprised Barry. He didn't think that she had any romantic thoughts anymore. "What about their relationship did you find 'dreamy,' as you put it?" he asked, still not looking at her.

Carol thought for a moment and said, "People who are having affairs seem to find the time to talk to each other. They call each other. They make plans to be together. They actually want to make each other happy. I don't know whether that guy in the movie really wanted to have a picnic on the beach, but he did it because she wanted to. It seems like people who are having affairs try harder to keep their relationship exciting."

Barry thought for a moment. "It doesn't seem like two people have to go outside their marriage to have an affair," Barry began. "A husband could have an affair with his wife. They wouldn't even have to sneak around or worry about getting caught."

Barry wasn't talking about their marriage. He was just saying that the writers could have put a married couple in an exciting relationship just as easily. But the moment the words were out of his mouth, he began thinking about the magnitude of his statement. He had incriminated his own marriage. As the impact of the statement struck him, Barry turned to look at Carol. By then, she was in tears. He pulled her close to him and held her as she wept. Finally he broke the ice and said, "I guess I haven't been a very romantic guy to be married to, have I?"

"It's not you," Carol said between the sobs. "It's us. We love each other . . . don't we?" She paused to look up at him for assurance.

"Of course we do," Barry reassured his wife. "We love each other. We just don't know how to be in love."

No longer crying, Carol continued, "I've allowed our sex life to become ho-hum because I just didn't know what to do. Look at us. We sit at opposite ends of the couch and watch other people have affairs."

Then Barry broke in with a thought. "What if we had an affair?"

"What!" Carol shot up in her seat and faced him.

"No!" Barry cut her off. "I mean, what if we decided to have an affair with each other?"

"Oh." Carol sat back, relaxed. "That's ridiculous."

Barry didn't agree, but he kept quiet. He felt as if he had an answer for their stagnant marriage and sex life. So he decided he was going to start pursuing his wife as if she were a woman married to someone else. No matter how hard she tried to avoid his advances, he was going to pursue this married woman. Even if she *was* married to him!

That was Monday night. Tuesday morning at 10:00, Barry called Carol at her office. The receptionist buzzed Carol's phone to say she had a call. "Who is it?" Carol asked the receptionist.

"Carol . . .," the receptionist hesitated. "When I asked him who he was, he said his name was Barry. I recognized his voice and said, 'Oh hi, Barry,' but he acted as if he didn't know me. I mean I think it's your husband, but he didn't act like your husband. Anyway, he said his name was Barry."

Carol picked up the phone a little bewildered and said, "Hello."

"Carol," said the voice she recognized as her husband's, "my name is Barry. I was at your office Christmas party last year with a friend of mine. She told me who you were, and I've been thinking about you ever since. I know we haven't been introduced yet, but I couldn't wait any longer to meet you. Will you meet me for lunch? I want to get to know you, and I want you to get to know me. Before you turn me down, let me say that I've already made reservations for two at Trader Vic's for twelve noon. I'll be waiting there in a blue suit and a red tie. I hope you won't disappoint me." Click.

They sat at lunch for an hour that day and just talked. Barry's attentiveness was reminiscent of their dating years; he was totally focused on her. As he walked her to her car he made one more announcement. "I called Elaine this morning and asked her if we could drop off the kids at 6:30. I have 7:00 dinner reservations at Winston's."

"Can we afford to do all this?" Carol asked.

"I'll be fine as long as my wife doesn't find out," Barry shouted back at her as he walked away. It was loud enough to embarrass her since several other people were in the parking lot, but she just got in her car and drove away smiling.

"What an idiot he is," Carol thought as she pulled back into her office parking lot. "But he's a romantic idiot!"

That night they sat at the restaurant for three hours. For the first time in years, they began to talk about their sex life. Finally, Carol giggled that she felt so uncomfortable. When Barry asked why, she said, "Well, I decided that I was going to get into this little game of yours, and I wanted to wear something that you would like."

Barry cut in with, "I noticed you wore my favorite dress. You look very sexy tonight."

"Not as sexy as I feel," Carol responded. "I left work a little early and stopped off at Victoria's Secret on the way home. I picked up something I think you'll like. . . . I'm wearing it underneath this dress. Two can play this game, you know."

Barry all but dropped his water in his lap.

"You used to hint about my getting something from Victoria's Secret, but I always felt too foolish and unsexy to walk in there. If we're going to have this 'affair,' I'm going to have to risk trying to seduce you. Unfortunately, all I've been thinking about is what would happen if we had an accident and my new black silk lingerie had to be cut off me. What a waste. . . ."

Barry's eyes opened wider and a grin slowly spread across his face. As Carol smiled back at him, they both realized they were now on the same page. The first page of a steamy novel about two people who were in the back corner of a restaurant, learning to love each other.

Where Do We Begin?

Barry and Carol decided to take several new steps in their relationship. First of all they decided to set a night each week to continue their discussion about their sex life. Barry actually started that conversation at the restaurant that night.

"When we were talking on the couch, I knew you were saying that our love life has gotten boring. I think we're moving in the right direction, but I still feel a little hesitant about bringing up specific issues with you. I'm not sure I know how far you are willing to go when it comes to experimenting with new things. You know, things like different positions."

"This is the first I've heard of this. Why haven't you ever asked me what I'd like to do?" Carol asked her husband as she reached across the table and slipped her hand under his. She noticed that he was staring down at the table as if this was a hard topic of discussion for him.

"Oh, but I have!" Barry responded, looking up. "I've tried to tell you, but you didn't seem interested."

"I guess when you've tried to do different things," Carol answered, "either I wasn't really sure what you were trying to get me to do, or I wasn't sure how much you wanted to do them. You always backed off so quickly. And I'll be honest. I was always a little scared to try new things. I felt like I wouldn't know how to do them right or that I'd look silly. Sometimes I thought you might want me to do things that I was uncomfortable with. Wearing my new lingerie tonight has made me a little nervous. It's all new territory."

That night Barry and Carol sat and discussed making their sex life more creative. It was the first time in their marriage that they talked about these things in a way that showed that each person was trying to find out what the other really wanted. That night as one person brought up different options, the other person listened.

Stop Right Here!

This is a great time to think about (if you're reading alone) or talk about (if you're reading this with your spouse) these things in your own marriage. What are some creative things you would like to try when you make love? Rather than just heading to bed at 11:00 to have sex, try putting into practice what you've just thought about or discussed.

That night, Barry and Carol had an in-depth discussion on foreplay. They agreed that there were some areas of foreplay that were absolutely out. They had friends who were watching X-rated videos, but they knew that was unacceptable for them. In fact, they discussed why they thought it was wrong to watch sexually explicit movies and videos, so that they were sure they were thinking the same things.

From there, they each went on to try define foreplay. First Carol talked about her concept of foreplay. Then she gave some examples of how foreplay could actually start at the supper table. This helped Barry understand that Carol viewed lovemaking as a long process rather than a brief biological encounter.

Stop Again!

At this point the wife should try to define an ideal evening of foreplay from her perspective. Start with saying "hello" to each other at the beginning of the evening and continue all the way up to intercourse. Perhaps it would help to do what Barry did. What would be exciting to do if you and your husband decided to have your own affair?

"I feel like making love when you come home at night and _____."

"On the other hand it turns me off when _____."

"This is why I get turned off: _____."

Barry was surprised to find out that there were some things that he did that Carol found to be demeaning. She told him that she felt like an object rather than a person when he patted her on the bottom when they were in public. "I know it's just a little thing," Carol said, "but it makes me feel like I'm one of those bikini-clad 'babes' who hang around the pool for the men to ogle. When the men are ready to talk business, she gets patted on the bottom, as a way of dismissing her from the area. I know that sounds so stupid, but that's how demeaned I feel when you pat me on the bottom in public." It didn't make any sense to Barry. In fact, he actually liked it when she used to place her hand in his back pocket, on his bottom, as they walked arm in arm through the mall. But he was beginning to realize that just because he liked it didn't mean that she liked it or that she should like it. They were different, and they were finally talking about those differences.

Next it was Barry's turn to talk about his definition of foreplay. They both discovered that he hadn't really thought much about nonsexual foreplay. Initially, for him, the issues were the desire to talk about oral sex or various positions. But as they talked, he realized that these weren't really foreplay. They were varieties of sexual play.

"Now that we're talking about it," Barry began to think out loud, "I guess that going out to this special dinner and talking about our sex life is very arousing for me. I guess I'd consider that foreplay. The fact that you told me about the sexy lingerie you have on is very arousing, so that would also be foreplay."

As they talked further, Carol began to realize that for Barry, visual stimuli played a big part. He got very excited about seeing her get undressed in front of him. That night they even discussed various clothes and nightgowns that turned him on.

Stop Again!

At this juncture the husband should try to describe what he thinks foreplay is. At what point do you believe the actual foreplay begins?_____
_____
_____.

If visual stimulation is a significant part of your definition of foreplay, what would you like to see your wife wearing or not wearing? _____.

At this first dinner discussion, an important door was permanently opened to discuss things that one spouse might want to do but the other spouse felt uncomfortable doing. Barry and Carol were finally able to talk about their sex life without battling. Each was finally willing to allow the other to bring up difficult topics. Barry wanted to talk about oral sex. Carol was uncomfortable with that topic, but for the first time she was willing to talk about her objections rather than to just say, "I don't want to talk about it." Barry listened to her reasons for objecting, and they discussed them. Barry didn't belittle her objections, and for the first time, Carol felt as if her opinion counted. She finally felt as if her feelings were more important to Barry than his desires.

Stop Again!

What topics are difficult for you to talk about?_____

_____

Why? How can you talk about them in a way that allows you to disagree?_____

_____

_____

Barry and Carol didn't change their whole sex life that night. But they did make a radical change in their love life. Their discussion was handled in a way that made each person feel like winning the issues was not the prime motive for the discussion. They felt as if they had grown closer because they were finally talking about their sexual feelings. More importantly, they were finally desiring to make love rather than have sex. Barry and Carol each made a commitment to try to figure out how to please each other. They also made a commitment not to push each other anymore. Instead they would discuss openly and listen patiently.

What About You?

Whether you're reading this book alone or, as we have suggested, out loud with your spouse, what steps can you take? What do you need to do to take the step from having sex to making love? This step is directional. You have to move away from seeing sex as a way of getting what you desire toward seeing sex as an opportunity to share ecstasy with your spouse. It doesn't come naturally. It will take time and effort. But what great work it can be!

Perhaps you just skipped over the previous questions in this chapter. They seemed too embarrassing or difficult to answer.

Choose a night and make an appointment to either get out of the house or take the phone off the hook and ship the kids out. It's time to answer those questions. Stop wasting valuable time. Be the spouse to start the process rolling. The only thing you have to lose is the time you spend sitting apart on that couch dreaming about it or wishing for it. Remember, making love is an attitude you adopt toward another person, not something you get from that other person. Go after it with great sexpectations! And God bless you as you seek his plan for your marriage.

Notes

Chapter 3
Myth: What You See Is What You Get

1. Clifford and Joyce Penner, "Women Want Sex Too," *Marriage Partnership* (Winter 1992).

Chapter 7
Myth: Good Sex Is When You Fill My Wish List

1. Clifford and Joyce Penner, *The Gift of Sex* (Waco: Word, 1981).
2. Edward Lauman, Stuart Michaels, Robert Michael and John Gagnon, *Sex In America: A Definitive Survey* (New York: Little, Brown, 1994).

Chapter 8
Myth: Good-bye Passion, Good-bye Love

1. Lauman et al., *Sex in America*.

Chapter 9
Myth: Couples Are Born Compatible

1. John D. Cunningham and John K. Antill, "Cohabitation and Marriage: Retrospective and Predictive Comparisons," *Journal of Social and Personal Relationships* 11 (1994): 77–93.
2. Robert Schoen and Robin M. Weinick, "Partner Choice in Marriages and Cohabitations," *Journal of Marriage and the Family* 55 (1993): 408–14.
3. Lauman et al., *Sex in America*.
4. James Talley and Bobbie Reed, *Too Close Too Soon* (Nashville: Thomas Nelson, 1990).

Chapter 10
Love in the Time of Children

1. Robert Barnes, *Who's in Charge Here* (Dallas: Word, 1989).

Chapter 13
When She's Not Interested

1. John Courtright and Sin Rogers, *Your Wife Was Sexually Abused* (Grand Rapids: Zondervan, 1994).

2. Marcel Waldinger, Michiel Hengeveld, Aeilko Zwinderman, "Paroxetine Treatment of Premature Ejaculation," *American Journal of Psychiatry* 151 (September 1994): 1377.

3. Penner, *The Gift of Sex.*

4. D. M. Purnine, "Gender Differences Regarding Preferences for Specific Heterosexual Practices," *Journal of Sex and Marital Therapy* 20 (Winter 1994): 271.

5. Marie Robinson, *The Power of Sexual Surrender* (New York: Signet Books, 1959).

Chapter 14
When He's Not Interested

1. J. P. Sneider, "How to Recognize the Signs of Sexual Addiction: Asking the Right Questions May Uncover Serious Problems," *Postgraduate Medicine* 90 (Nov. 1991): 171.

Chapter 15
Learning to Love

1. Purnine, "Gender Differences," 271.

For More Information

Dr. Robert and Rosemary Barnes have written other books that will help your family. These books can be purchased or ordered from a bookstore near you.

Single Parenting: A Practical Guide to Walk Your Child into Adulthood

Raising Confident Kids

Who's in Charge Here: Overcoming Power Struggles with Your Child

You're Not My Daddy: Winning the Heart of Your Stepchild

Rock-Solid Marriage: Building a Permanent Relationship in a Throw-Away World

We Need to Talk: Opening Doors of Communication with Your Mate

The Barneses also conduct parenting or marriage seminars all across North America. For more information on the seminars, books, or tapes, please call 1–800–838–1552 or write:

Dr. Robert Barnes
Sheridan House Family Ministries
4200 S.W. 54 Ct.
Ft. Lauderdale, FL 33314